Practical Glimpse

Learn to Edit and Create Digital Photos and Art with This Powerful Open Source Image Editor

Phillip Whitt

Apress®

Practical Glimpse

Phillip Whitt
Columbus, GA, USA

ISBN-13 (pbk): 978-1-4842-6326-6   ISBN-13 (electronic): 978-1-4842-6327-3
https://doi.org/10.1007/978-1-4842-6327-3

Managing Director, Apress Media LLC: Welmoed Spahr
Acquisitions Editor: Louise Corrigan
Development Editor: James Markham
Coordinating Editor: Nancy Chen

Cover designed by eStudioCalamar

Cover image designed by TBD

Distributed to the book trade worldwide by Springer Science+Business Media New York, 1 New York Plaza, New York, NY 10004. Phone 1-800-SPRINGER, fax (201) 348-4505, e-mail orders-ny@springer-sbm.com, or visit www.springeronline.com. Apress Media, LLC is a California LLC and the sole member (owner) is Springer Science + Business Media Finance Inc (SSBM Finance Inc). SSBM Finance Inc is a **Delaware** corporation.

For information on translations, please e-mail booktranslations@springernature.com; for reprint, paperback, or audio rights, please e-mail bookpermissions@springernature.com.

Apress titles may be purchased in bulk for academic, corporate, or promotional use. eBook versions and licenses are also available for most titles. For more information, reference our Print and eBook Bulk Sales web page at http://www.apress.com/bulk-sales.

Any source code or other supplementary material referenced by the author in this book is available to readers on GitHub via the book's product page, located at www.apress.com/9781484263266. For more detailed information, please visit http://www.apress.com/source-code.

Printed on acid-free paper

This book is dedicated to my family and friends—thank you always for your support and encouragement.

Table of Contents

About the Author

Phillip Whitt is an author, photo retouch professional, and graphic designer. He is the author of several Apress books and video tutorials pertaining to image editing using GIMP and Adobe Photoshop Elements. He has edited, retouched, and restored countless digital images since the late 1990s. He has served both clients from the general public and a number of commercial clients over the years. In addition to over 20 years of image editing and graphic design experience, he also has an Expert Rating Certification in Adobe Photoshop Skills and VTC certifications in GIMP and Scribus.

About the Technical Reviewer

Seth Kenlon is a multimedia artist, free culture advocate, Linux geek, and D&D nerd. He has worked on indie and studio movies, including *Deadpool, Hunt for the Wilderpeople,* and *Guardians of the Galaxy 2*. He's worked in the computing industry for Apple creating bespoke RISC rendering tests, Red Hat, and IBM. He is one of the maintainers of the Slackware-based multimedia production project (`http://slackermedia.info`).

Acknowledgments

I'd like to first thank Louise Corrigan and Nancy Chen, both of whom I always enjoy working with. They are both first-rate professionals, and each one a credit to Apress. I'd also like to acknowledge everyone involved in the production of this book; your work is forever appreciated!

Introduction

Thank you for your interest in this book. It's written primarily to acquaint the reader with the most important aspects of Glimpse to help them start using it quickly. Throughout this book, there are a total of 35 step-by-step tutorials that can be used with the digital work files provided—they can be downloaded from the Apress website (`https://www.apress.com/9781484263266`) by clicking the Download Source Code button.

What Is Glimpse?

Glimpse is a powerful, open source image editing program. Glimpse is a fork of the popular program GIMP (an acronym for *GNU Image Manipulation Program*), meaning it uses the same base source code but is maintained by its own group of developers. Although (at this time) it's virtually identical to GIMP in most respects, it is a separate project. To see the Glimpse website, just click here: `https://glimpse-editor.org/`.

Why Was Glimpse Created?

GIMP is a free, open source image editing program. It's used by many graphic designers, web designers, digital illustrators, photographers—just about anyone who frequently works with digital images. Because GIMP is such a powerful program, it's often used as an alternative to Adobe Photoshop.

However, the name GIMP has been somewhat problematic for some. According to the Glimpse development team, the word *gimp* is a slur against a physically disabled person in some countries. It can also be meant as an insult to unpopular school children. To read more about their views on this matter, just click here: `https://glimpse-editor.org/about/#what-is-wrong-with-the-gimp-name`.

One especially good point made by the Glimpse development team is that educational and business environments unwilling to adopt GIMP because of the name might be willing to use Glimpse—this would be advantageous to schools or businesses constrained by limited budgets. Any potential negativity the GIMP name could cause would be eliminated by using Glimpse.

What Can Glimpse Do?

Glimpse, like GIMP or Photoshop, is used to modify, enhance, and retouch digital photos. It can be used to digitally repair and restore damaged old family photographs, or prepare images for use in marketing and other business materials.

One example of a useful feature is the *Shadows-Highlights* dialog, which is used to adjust dark and light parts of the image. Figure 1 shows an example of an image being enhanced using this feature by lightening the foreground.

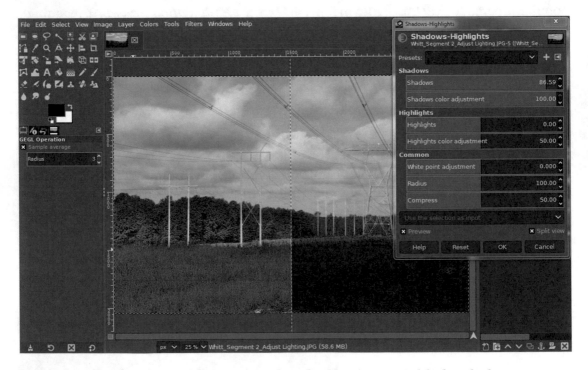

Figure 1. *The foreground lightened using the Shadows-Highlights dialog*

Glimpse is also used to create digital artwork. There is a wide array of tools for drawing, painting, and creating shapes. Figure 2 shows an illustration created from scratch using Glimpse.

Figure 2. *This illustration was created from scratch using Glimpse*

Glimpse is also useful for creating art from photos by using filters and experimenting with layer blend modes. The example in Figure 3 is the result of combining two images resulting in a digital mural.

Figure 3. *This image was created by combining two photos applying an artistic filter and using the Hard Light layer blend mode*

INTRODUCTION

This book covers Glimpse 0.1.2, which is based on GIMP 2.10.12. While this book was in the late stages of production, Glimpse was updated to version 0.2.0. The download and installation instructions in Chapter 1 have been updated accordingly. One of the major changes made is that many of the program's tools are now nested, resulting in a less cluttered toolbox. The tools are still there, they just aren't visible until the icon displaying a small triangle is clicked. For example, clicking the Clone tool icon reveals the Clone tool, Perspective Clone tool and Heal tool. Another notable update is that the 64-bit version of Glimpse for Windows now includes G'MIC (Greyc's Magic for Image Computing), an open-source framework for image processing. For more information about G'MIC, visit `https://gmic.eu`.

Now that you're introduced to Glimpse and some of its abilities (and hopefully, you're intrigued) and ready to start, let's move on to the first chapter.

PART I

Acquiring, Installing, and Getting to Know Glimpse

CHAPTER 1

An Overview of Glimpse

Are you ready to enter the world of digital image editing and give this powerful program a try? Great! This chapter will guide you in a few things to help you get up and running.

Note Before getting too far ahead, it should be mentioned that Glimpse does not work on Mac OS at this time. However, the GNU Image Manipulation Program (which is the program Glimpse is based on) does. The content in this book applies to this program equally well.

Here are the topics that will be covered in this chapter:

1. Downloading and installing Glimpse

2. An overview of the workspace

3. Customizing the workspace

4. Menus, windows, and dialogs

Now, let's proceed to the first topic.

Downloading and Installing Glimpse

To acquire Glimpse, you'll need to first go to the official website `https://www.glimpse-editor.github.io`. Once you've navigated to the home page, you'll find the download button (Figure 1-1).

© Phillip Whitt 2020
P. Whitt, *Practical Glimpse*, https://doi.org/10.1007/978-1-4842-6327-3_1

Figure 1-1. *The download button is easy to find on the Glimpse home page*

After clicking the download button, you'll be taken to the Downloads page. Glimpse runs on Windows 7 or later (32 or 64 bit). It also runs on Linux systems. It does not run on Mac OS at this time, but the GNU Image Manipulation Program does—if you use a Mac running this program, the content in this book applies just as well.

Installing Glimpse on Windows

The following steps will help guide you in the installation of Glimpse Image Editor on Windows from the Downloads page:

1. From the *Downloads* page (under the Windows subheading) ,
    click *Direct download link* shown in Figure 1-2.

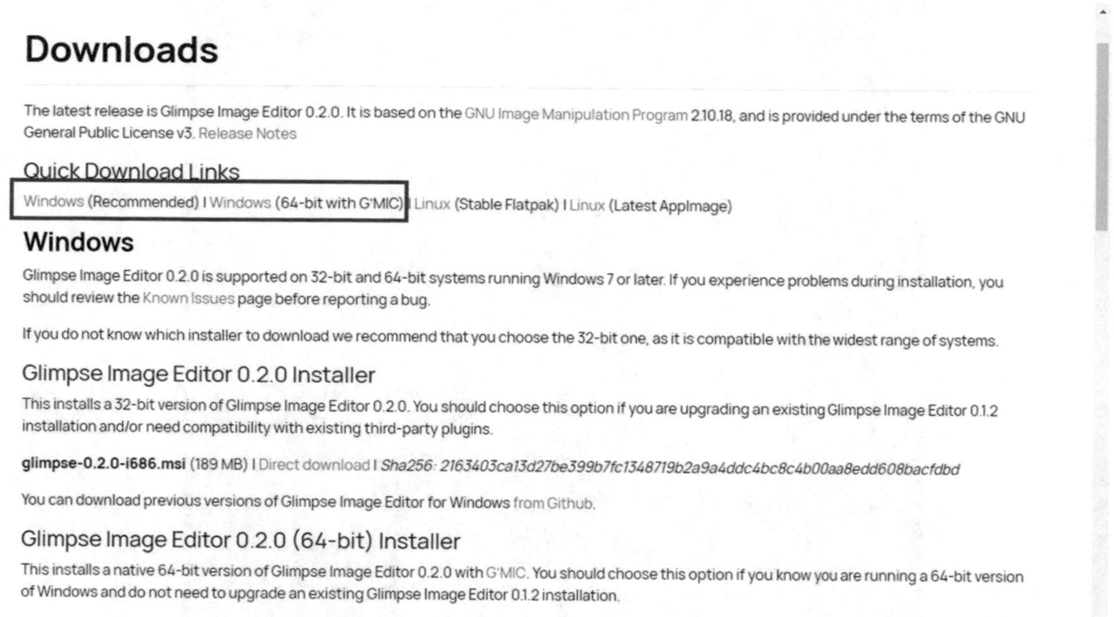

Downloads

The latest release is Glimpse Image Editor 0.2.0. It is based on the GNU Image Manipulation Program 2.10.18, and is provided under the terms of the GNU General Public License v3. Release Notes

Quick Download Links

Windows (Recommended) I Windows (64-bit with G'MIC) I Linux (Stable Flatpak) I Linux (Latest AppImage)

Windows

Glimpse Image Editor 0.2.0 is supported on 32-bit and 64-bit systems running Windows 7 or later. If you experience problems during installation, you should review the Known Issues page before reporting a bug.

If you do not know which installer to download we recommend that you choose the 32-bit one, as it is compatible with the widest range of systems.

Glimpse Image Editor 0.2.0 Installer

This installs a 32-bit version of Glimpse Image Editor 0.2.0. You should choose this option if you are upgrading an existing Glimpse Image Editor 0.1.2 installation and/or need compatibility with existing third-party plugins.

glimpse-0.2.0-i686.msi (189 MB) I Direct download I *Sha256: 2163403ca13d27be399b7fc1348719b2a9a4ddc4bc8c4b00aa8edd608bacfdbd*

You can download previous versions of Glimpse Image Editor for Windows from Github.

Glimpse Image Editor 0.2.0 (64-bit) Installer

This installs a native 64-bit version of Glimpse Image Editor 0.2.0 with G'MIC. You should choose this option if you know you are running a 64-bit version of Windows and do not need to upgrade an existing Glimpse Image Editor 0.1.2 installation.

Figure 1-2. *The Direct download link for Windows is shown outlined in red*

2. After the download is complete, the Glimpse 0.1.2 installer package can be found in *Downloads directory* (Figure 1-3).

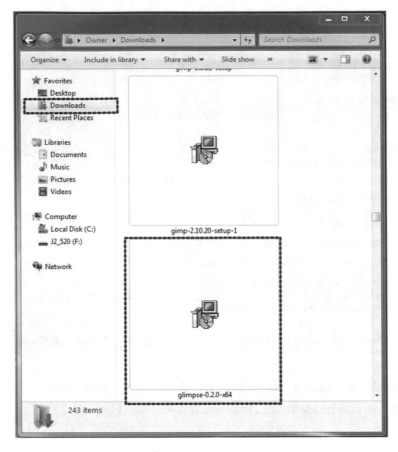

Figure 1-3. *The Glimpse installer located in the Downloads directory*

3. Double-click the installer package icon.

4. After the installer window launches, click the *Run* button when prompted.

5. The Glimpse Image Editor will then install on your Windows computer (Figure 1-4).

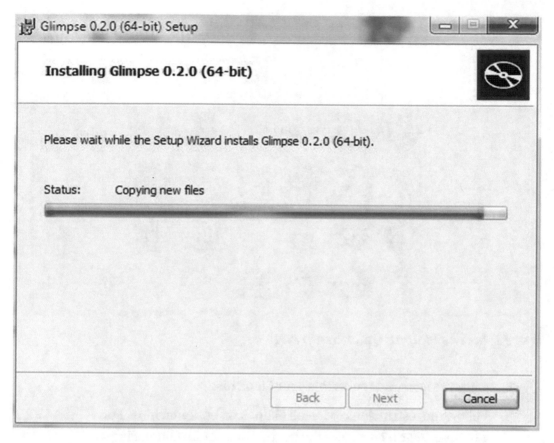

Figure 1-4. *The Glimpse Image Editor installation in progress*

Installing Glimpse on Linux

For Linux users, follow this guide to install Glimpse on your machine:

1. First, Flatpak (which can be used with over 22 distros) will need to be installed on your computer. If it's already installed on your machine, skip to step 4—if not, just follow the instructions found here: https://flatpak.org/setup/. You'll be taken to the *Quick Setup* page shown in Figure 1-5.

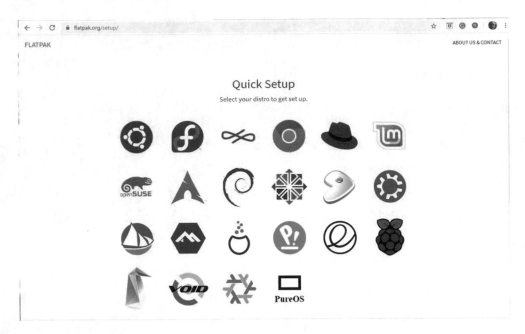

Figure 1-5. *The Flatpak Quick Setup page*

2. Click the icon that represents your Linux distro.

3. Follow the instructions to install Flatpak on your machine. For example, Figure 1-6 shows the instructions for installing Flatpak on Ubuntu (the installation instructions vary depending on which Linux distro you're using).

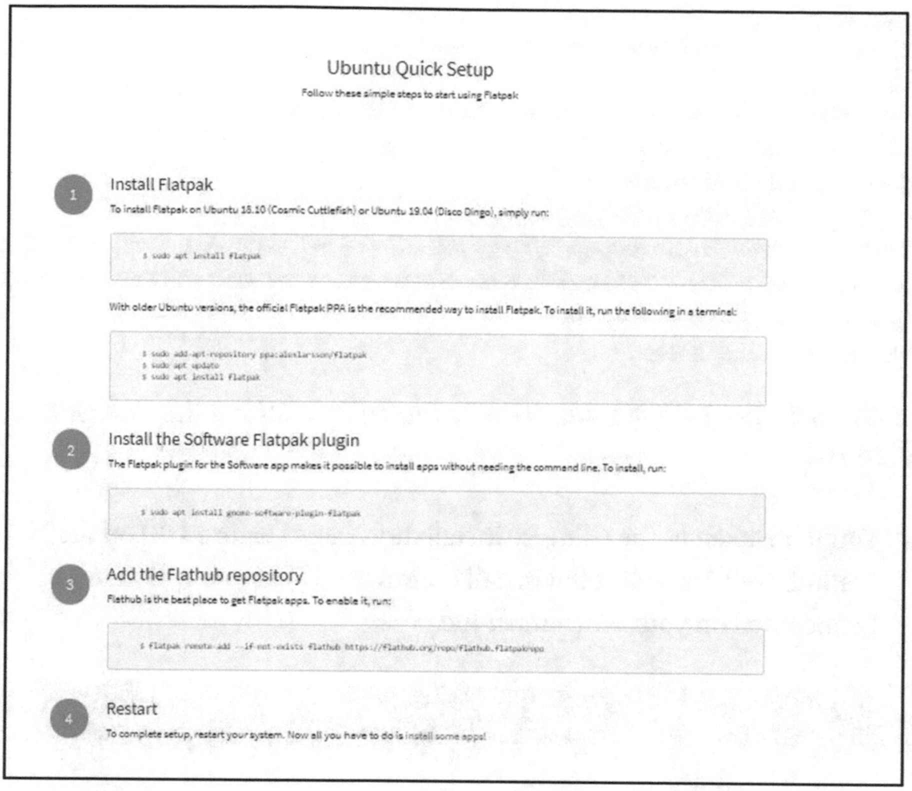

Figure 1-6. *Instructions for installing Flatpak will vary depending on which Linux distro is used*

4.   After Flatpak has been installed on your system (or if it's already
     supplied with your Linux distro), click the link (outlined in red) on
     the Glimpse Image Editor Downloads page (`https://glimpse-editor.github.io/downloads/`) shown in Figure 1-7.

Figure 1-7.   *Glimpse Image Editor can be found by clicking the link shown outlined in red*

5.   You'll be taken to the Glimpse installation page (Figure 1-8) on the Flathub website—click the Install button, and Glimpse will then be installed on your Linux machine.

Figure 1-8.   *The Download on Flathub button (outlined in red)*

Customizing the Workspace

After Glimpse Image Editor has been installed on your computer, you can then launch it to begin to familiarize yourself with the program. Figure 1-9 shows the Glimpse startup screen.

Figure 1-9. *The Glimpse Image Editor startup screen*

Single- and Multi-window Modes

By default, the Glimpse interface launches in the single-window mode (meaning all the panels are anchored to the Active Image Window). It also opens in the Dark theme by default, as shown in Figure 1-10.

Figure 1-10. *The default Glimpse interface*

The interface can be resized by clicking and dragging one of the edges or corners.

For users who prefer floating panels, Glimpse can function in a multi-window mode by deactivating the single-window mode from the Windows menu (Figure 1-11).

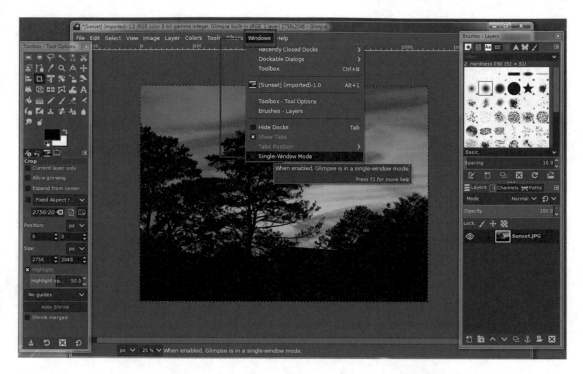

Figure 1-11. *Deactivating the single-window mode initiates a multi-window mode, allowing the docks to be moved if desired*

When working in the multi-window mode, it's easy to accidentally close a dock when the intention is to close the entire program. When this occurs, the dock can be reopened from the Image Menu:

Windows ➤ Recently Closed Docks (Figure 1-12).

Figure 1-12. *An accidentally closed dock can be reopened from the Image Menu*

Themes

Dark interface themes have become widely used in many image editing programs over the past several years. Glimpse opens in the Dark theme by default; it can be changed from Dark to Light if desired (Figure 1-13).

Figure 1-13. *The Glimpse interface shown in the Light theme*

To change the theme from Dark to Light:

1. Go to Edit ➤ Preferences.

2. The Preferences dialog will open.

3. Click Theme in the Preferences dialog, then click Light in the Select Theme sub-menu (Figure 1-14).

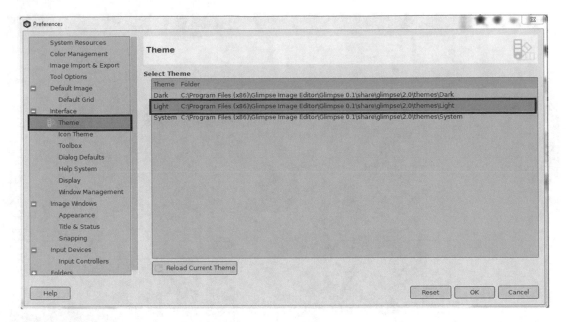

Figure 1-14. *The Glimpse theme is changed in the Preferences dialog*

Icon Themes

There are several icon themes in Glimpse Image Editor (while this book was in the late stages of production, the Glimpse team added additional icon themes that are not pictured here). Icon themes can be changed in the Preferences dialog. The icon themes are as follows:

- **Legacy**—These were used in older versions of the GNU Image Manipulation Program. There is also an option for color icons (not shown).

- **Symbolic**—The default icons used in Glimpse. There is also an option for Symbolic-high contrast icons (not shown).

- **Symbolic Inverted**—Essentially, these are "negatives" of the Symbolic icons (best viewed using the Light theme). There is also an option for Symbolic Inverted-high contrast icons (not shown).

Figure 1-15 shows a comparison of the different Icon themes.

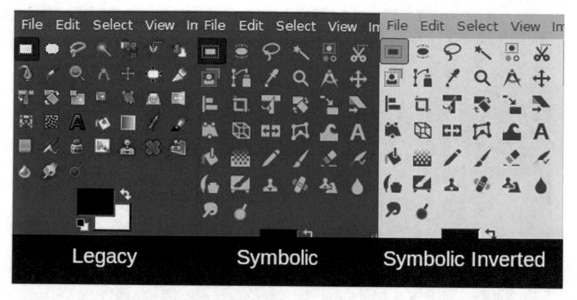

Figure 1-15. *A comparison of the Glimpse Icon themes (not shown are Color, Symbolic-High Contrast, or Symbolic Inverted-High Contrast)*

To change the Icon Theme:

1. Go to Edit ➤ Preferences.

2. The Preferences dialog will open.

3. Click Icon Theme in the Preferences dialog, then click the icon
    theme you desire in the Icon Theme submenu as shown in
    Figure 1-16.

Figure 1-16. *The Icon Theme is changed in the Preferences dialog*

Windows and Menus

Because Glimpse Image Editor is so powerful and complex, we'll now have a quick overview of the menus, windows, and dialogs. This is to help beginners get a general sense of where to find the tools, features, and functions that are offered in this program. They will be covered in greater detail in later chapters.

The Active Image Window and Status Bar

This Active Image Window displays the currently active image. The Status Bar is located just below (Figure 1-17).

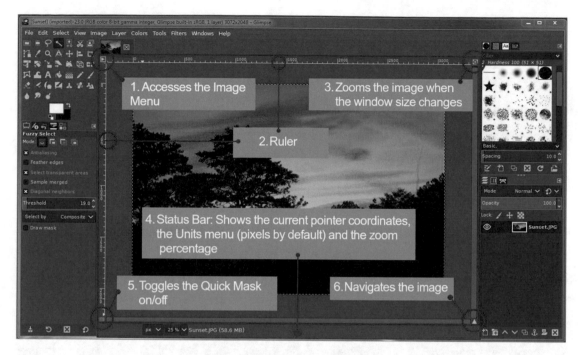

Figure 1-17. *The Active Image Window and Status Bar*

There are several functions available from the Active Image Window and Status Bar:

1. **Access the Image Menu (Triangular Button)**—Opens the Image
   Menu displayed as a column.

2. **Ruler/Guides**—Scale that runs horizontally along the top and
   vertically along the left side of the image. Displays units in pixels
   by default, but the units can be changed by accessing the Units
   menu on the Status Bar. Guides can be dragged from both the
   vertical and horizontal rulers and are used to help in placement of
   graphical elements.

3. **Zooms When the Window Size Changes (Zoom Icon)**—When
   enabled, the active image zooms as the window is resized.

4. **Status Bar** (located just below the Active Image Window)—
   Displays the current cursor/pointer coordinates, the Units menu
   (which shows dimensions in pixels by default), and the zoom
   percentage of the active image.

5. **Toggles the Quick Mask On/Off (Shift+Q)**—Displays a translucent overlay (outside of a selection) over the active image, allowing the user to make precise refinements to the selection (this will be covered in greater detail in a later chapter).

6. **Navigates the Image**—By clicking and holding this button, the user can easily navigate around the active image by dragging in a small preview window.

The Title Bar

The Title Bar is located at the top of the Glimpse interface. If no image is open, it simply reads Glimpse. When an image is open, it displays the image name, whether it's new or imported, the color mode, the color profile, and dimensions (Figure 1-18).

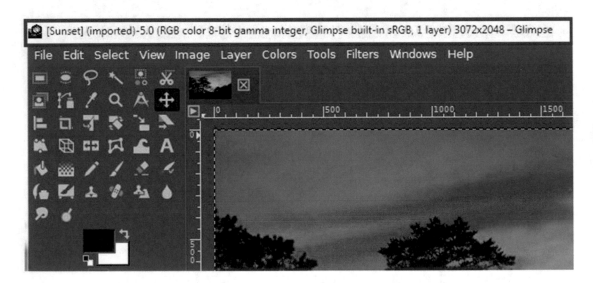

Figure 1-18. *The Title Bar shown on top of the Glimpse interface*

The Image Menu

The Image Menu is perpetually displayed just below the Title Bar. This could be thought of as "Command Center," where most of the program's functions can be accessed. As briefly mentioned earlier, the Image Menu (displayed in a column) can also be opened and closed from the triangular button in the upper-left corner of the Main Image Window (Figure 1-19).

Figure 1-19. *The Image Menu shown outlined in red*

When an option is selected from the Image Menu (e.g., File), a dialog box opens. By holding the cursor over a function, a small call-out window appears describing the function's purpose (Figure 1-20). The *Create* and *Open New* functions are accompanied by the ➤ angle bracket symbol and contain submenus with additional functions.

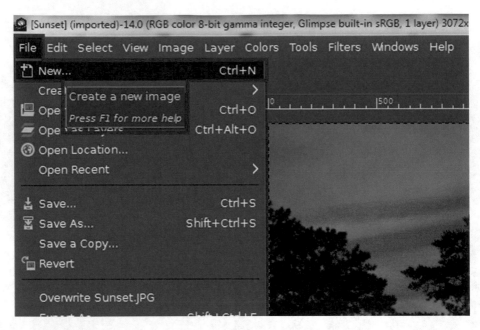

Figure 1-20. *Holding the cursor over a function displays a small call-out window describing the function's purpose*

The Image Navigation Bar

The Image Navigation allows you to easily navigate through the open images in Glimpse, which are represented as thumbnail images (Figure 1-21). Click the thumbnail of the image you want to display in the Main Image Window.

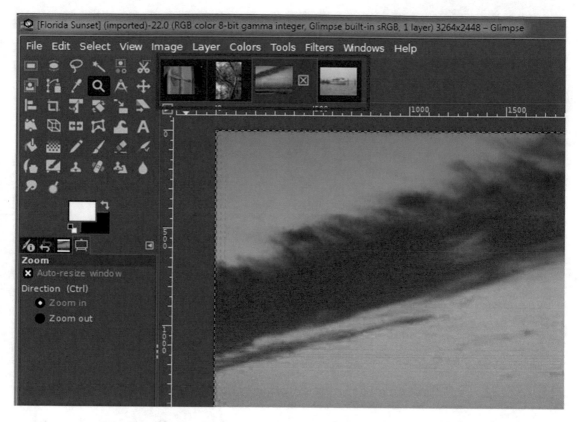

Figure 1-21. *The Image Navigation bar allows the user to navigate the open images*

Dialogs, Docks, and Tabs

Dialogs are windows that provide options for adjusting the settings of a specific tool, function, and so on. Figure 1-22 shows the Toolbox with the Tool Options Dialog open. Here, the tool settings can be adjusted to suit the task at hand. The Toolbox and Tool Options will be covered in greater detail in Chapter 3.

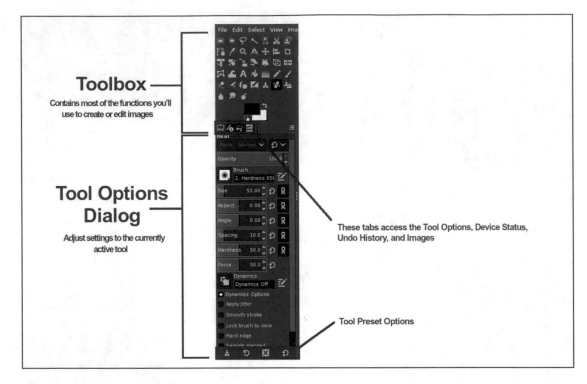

Figure 1-22. *The Toolbox and the Tool Options Dialog*

Docks essentially contain multiple dialogs in a single panel. Figure 1-23 shows the Brushes Dialog and the Layers Dialog unified in a dock.

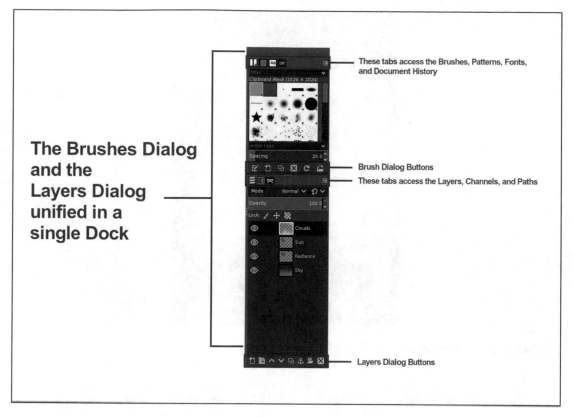

Figure 1-23. *The Brushes Dialog and the Layers Dialog contained in a dock*

Tabs (resembling file-folder tabs) provide access to various dialogs contained within a dock. Clicking a particular tab makes that dialog active. Figure 1-24 shows the Brushes Tab and the active dialog (outlined in red). Hovering the cursor over the tab displays a small call-out window with the dialog's name.

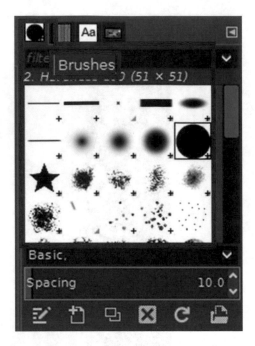

Figure 1-24. *The Brushes Tab and active dialog*

If desired, tabs can be dragged and detached from one dock and attached to another. This allows the user to further customize the Glimpse interface. Figure 1-25 shows the *Brushes Dialog* being dragged from its default location to the dock on the left side of the Glimpse interface.

Figure 1-25. *The Brushes Dialog being dragged from its default location to another dock*

The Configure Tab Dialog launches a menu allowing the user to select from numerous options related to the dialog (Figure 1-26).

Figure 1-26. *The Configure Tab button launches a menu displaying numerous options*

Opening, Saving, and Exporting Files

Glimpse is capable of working with a wide variety of file types, including common formats such as JPEG, PNG, and TIFF. It even offers partial compatibility with files such as PaintShop Pro (open only) and Photoshop (open and export).

Opening, saving, and exporting files can be done from the File Menu, although some of these actions can be handled using keyboard shortcuts.

Note   Like the GNU Image Manipulation Program, Glimpse handles saving and exporting files a bit differently than other image editing programs. These functions will be briefly covered in this part of the chapter.

Opening Files

There are several options available for opening a file. Figure 1-27 shows an example of using the Open option in the File Menu to locate an image stored on the computer.

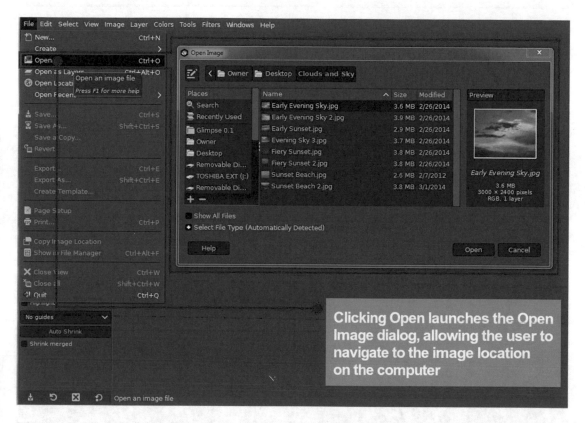

Figure 1-27. *Clicking Open launches a dialog allowing the user to navigate to the image stored on the computer*

The options for opening files in Glimpse are as follows:

- **Open (Ctrl+O)**—Opens an image file stored on your computer's hard drive, external hard drive, or other means of storage.

- **Open as Layers (Ctrl+Alt+O)**—Opens an image file and places it atop an active image as a layer.

- **Open Location**—Opens an image file from a web page by entering or copying and pasting the URL in the dialog window.

- **Open Recent**—Displays a submenu listing the most files that have been opened in Glimpse. The Document History dialog can be opened from the bottom of the submenu to find files opened further back in time.

Tip   If for some reason Open Location fails to work, a simple work-around is to right-click the image hosted on the web page and save it to your computer; then you'll be able to open it into Glimpse (be sure to respect copyright laws).

Saving Files

When saving an image in Glimpse, it uses the XCF file extension—this is the native file format for both the GNU Image Manipulation Program and Glimpse. When creating projects with multiple layers, saving your work preserves all of the layers and layer properties (Figure 1-28).

Figure 1-28.   *Glimpse saves your work in the .XCF format, preserving layers and layer properties*

The options for opening files in Glimpse are as follows:

- **Save (Ctrl+S)**—Saves the currently active image; initially, a dialog will display prompting the user to name the image, and select which folder it should be saved.

- **Save As (Shift+Ctrl+S)**—Saves the image with a different name.

- **Save a Copy**—Saves a copy of the image without affecting the source file or the state of the currently active image.

- **Revert**—Discards all of the changes made and reloads the original file from the disc.

Exporting Files

Exporting files allows the user to save images in file formats other than the .XCF format. There are many choices of file formats available, including the Adobe Photoshop extension .PSD (offering partial compatibility). In Figure 1-29, an .XCF image is being exported as a JPEG file. The .XCF file remains unchanged until edited further.

Figure 1-29. *Exporting an image in the .XCF file as a JPEG file*

The options for exporting files in Glimpse are as follows:

- **Export/Export To (Ctrl+E)**—Saves a file under a different file extension. After an image has been exported and editing continues, the option reads *Export to*, followed by the image name.

- **Export As (Shift+Ctrl+E)**—Launches the *Export Image* dialog, allowing the user to select from a list of file extensions.

Chapter Conclusion

This chapter provided an overview of Glimpse—everything from downloading it, installing it, and a look at the interface with its various menus and dialogs.

Here are the main topics that were covered:

- Downloading and installing Glimpse

- Customizing the workspace

- Windows and menus

- Opening, saving, and exporting files

In the next chapter, we'll cover Layers, Channels, Paths, and Undo History.

CHAPTER 2

Layers, Channels, Paths, and Undo History

Now that you've had a tour of the Glimpse interface, we'll look closer at some important aspects of Glimpse and how they relate to image editing.

The topics covered in this chapter are

1. An overview of layers

2. An overview of RGB color channels

3. An overview of paths

4. An overview of Undo History

An Overview of Layers

Layers are important in image editing—they make the life of the Glimpse user much easier! Layers allow corrections, revisions, and other edits to be made without scrapping the image and starting over from scratch. Layers also allow more flexibility by utilizing various *Blend Modes*, which we'll touch on in a later chapter.

Layer Basics

Layers can be thought of as transparent sheets containing graphical elements—each layer might have one or more elements. The combination of all the layers forms a complete image (Figure 2-1).

© Phillip Whitt 2020
P. Whitt, *Practical Glimpse*, https://doi.org/10.1007/978-1-4842-6327-3_2

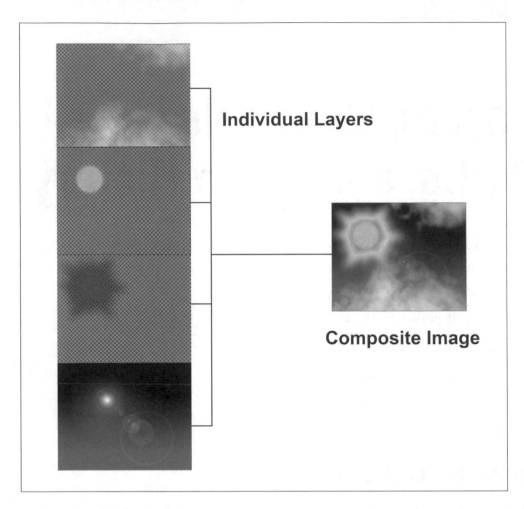

Figure 2-1. *Layers are comparable to transparent sheets containing graphical elements that, when combined, form a complete image*

The stacking order of layers can be changed or graphical elements can be added, removed, repositioned, or modified. This allows the user to exercise a great deal of control over the image being worked with.

In the old days of digital image editing (before the existence of layers), the work was done on a single, base image. If revisions were necessary, it usually required starting over from scratch (or, at the very least, encountering great difficulty when making revisions).

As mentioned a little earlier, layers offer the user much greater control over the editing process—if a mistake is made, the offending layer can be modified or discarded without affecting the rest of the image.

One example of how layers make life easier is it allows one to evaluate the work as it progresses and modify it when needed. For example, if I want to view the image without the clouds, clicking the eye-shaped icon in the *Layers Dialog* hides the layer's visibility (Figure 2-2). It also renders the layer inactive—the layer is removed from the image without actually being discarded. Clicking the eye-shaped icon again reactivates the layer and its visibility.

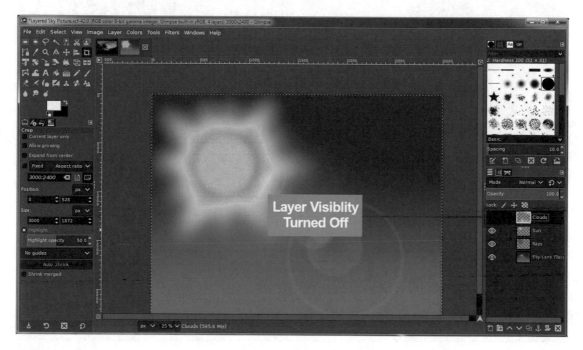

Figure 2-2. *Clicking the eye-shaped icon hides the layer's visibility*

Layers can be repositioned by using the *Move Tool* or the arrow keys. Figure 2-3 shows the layer containing the clouds has been repositioned slightly. The border of the layer is indicated by the dashed yellow and black outline.

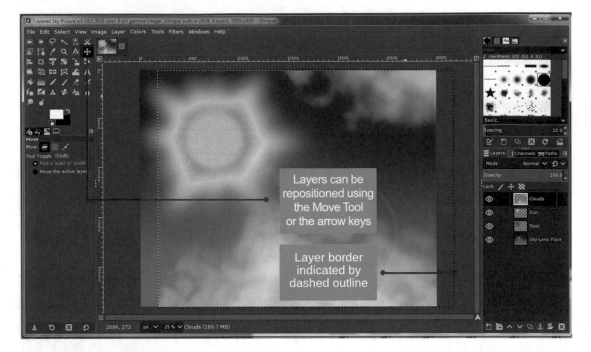

Figure 2-3. *Layers can be repositioned using the Move Tool or the arrow keys*

Note   If you'll notice, the repositioned layer's border doesn't line up with the rest of the image. By right-clicking the layer and selecting *Layer to Image Size* from the menu, the layer will be resized, and its border will match the rest of the image.

Layers can be drawn or painted on using the brush tools, or portions of the layer can be removed using the Eraser Tool.

Organizing Layers

Complex images may contain ten, twenty, or even dozens of layers. Using Glimpse, you can add as many layers to your project as your computer's disc space can handle. When an image contains many layers, it's important to manage them. Layers can be organized according to related graphical elements. The layers used in the illustration shown in Figure 2-4 are organized by using *Color Tags*—the layers containing mountains are tagged in blue, the layers containing the stars and moon are tagged in green, and the ones containing the clouds are tagged in yellow.

Figure 2-4. *Using Color Tags helps keep organize layers containing related elements*

This helps keep track of layers in more complex images and makes it easier to locate a specific layer when necessary.

Note   Color Tags can be added when launching the *Create a New Layer* dialog, or if the layer has already been created, double-clicking the layer thumbnail launches the *Layer Attributes* dialog and a Color Tag can be added then.

Layer Groups help keep layers managed as a list; this is useful for grouping layers that are similar or if you want to group layers that comprise an object in an image—this is especially useful if it's a complex image many layers are involved. In Figure 2-5, all the layers that comprise the TV set are in a group.

Figure 2-5. *The layers that comprise the TV set are in a layer group*

The Layer Group can be collapsed, thus hiding the layers keeping the Layers Dialog more tidy. This is done by clicking the small +/– icon next to the layer group thumbnail preview (Figure 2-6).

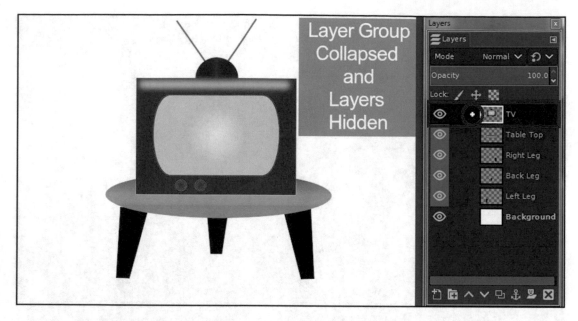

Figure 2-6. *The layer group collapsed and the layers hidden*

Layer Masks

A layer mask can be added to an active layer, allowing selective, nondestructive adjustment of the layer's opacity (or transparency). While a layer's opacity can be adjusted on a global (overall) level using the Opacity slider in the Layers Dialog, a layer mask allows the user to adjust opacity or transparency on selected areas with precision.

A layer mask is added by right-clicking the layer you want to add it to and selecting *Add Layer Mask* from the menu; you can also click the *Add Layer Mask* icon on the bottom of the Layers Dialog. This launches the *Add Layer Mask* menu where the Layer Mask properties are set (Figure 2-7).

Figure 2-7. *The layer mask properties are set in the Add Layer Mask menu*

The image of the yellow and purple flowers shown in Figure 2-8 contains two layers—the top layer is a duplicate of the bottom one, but it has been *desaturated* (color removed).

Figure 2-8. *A layer mask allows selective, nondestructive adjustment of layer transparency*

In this example, by adding a layer mask (initialized to white), selected areas can be made transparent by painting with black, revealing the color from the bottom layer. Painting in gray creates semitransparency, allowing some of the color to show through— the lighter the gray, the less color is revealed.

Using a layer mask offers nondestructive editing; opacity can be restored by painting with white if revisions are necessary.

Note   The layer mask must be active to work—to make the layer mask active, click the layer mask thumbnail image in the Layers Dialog.

The Layers Dialog and Layer Menus

By default, the Layers Dialog is located to the right of the Active Image Window. The layer order is displayed by *thumbnail images* (small preview images). The Layers Dialog contains a number of functions available for layer management (Figure 2-9).

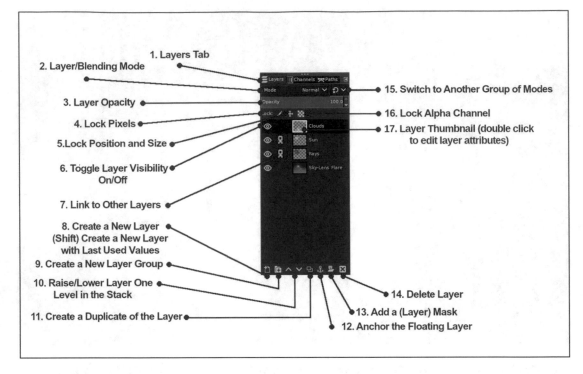

Figure 2-9. *The Layers Dialog*

The Layers Dialog's functions are as follows:

1. **Layers Tab**—Activates the Layers Dialog when clicked.

2. **Mode (Blend Mode)**—Selects from the 21 blend modes available (blend modes affect the way layers interact, or "blend" with each other).

3. **Layer Opacity**—Slider that adjusts the layer's opacity from 0% (completely transparent) through 100% (completely opaque).

4. **Lock Pixels**—Prevents the use of any brush-based tool on the layer's content, protecting it from any unwanted changes.

5. **Lock Position and Size**—When active, prevents the layer from being repositioned, resized, rotated, or otherwise transformed.

6. **Toggle Visibility On/Off**—Turns the layer visibility on or off; when toggled off, the layer is inactive and can't be edited.

7. **Link to Other Layers**—Allows layers to be linked together, allowing them to be moved, resized, rotated, or transformed uniformly; a chain link icon is visible next to each linked layer thumbnail image.

8. **Create a New Layer**—Launches the *New Layer* dialog, allowing the user to set the layer parameters before adding it to the image; holding the Shift key while clicking creates a new layer with the previously used values.

9. **Create a New Layer Group**—Creates a Layer Group, which enables the user to group similar layers in a tree list.

10. **Raise/Lower Layer One Level in Stack**—Moves the active layer up or down one level each time the up or down arrow is clicked; the layer can also be moved by clicking and dragging the thumbnail image up or down in the layer stack.

11. **Create a Duplicate of the Layer**—Creates a duplicate of the active layer.

12. **Anchor the Floating Layer**—Anchors the floating selection to the layer one level below.

13. **Add a Mask**—Launches the Add Layer Mask menu; the parameters can be set before the mask is added to the active layer.

14. **Delete Layer**—Discards the active layer.

15. **Switch to Another Group of Modes**—Switches between the default blend modes and the legacy blend modes (used in older versions of the GNU Image Manipulation Program).

16. **Lock Alpha Channel**—Prevents pixels from being applied to transparent parts of the layer.

17. **Layer Thumbnail**—*A small preview image of the layer(s) in the Layers Dialog; double-clicking in the thumbnail launches the Layer Attributes menu.*

The Layer Menu can be accessed from the Image Menu (Image Menu ➤ Layer). In Figure 2-10, you can see several of the options in the Layers Dialog are found also in this menu. In addition, there are options for managing the layer stacking order, layer mask, transparency, transforming the layer (flipping, rotating) and adjusting the boundary size, scaling, and cropping.

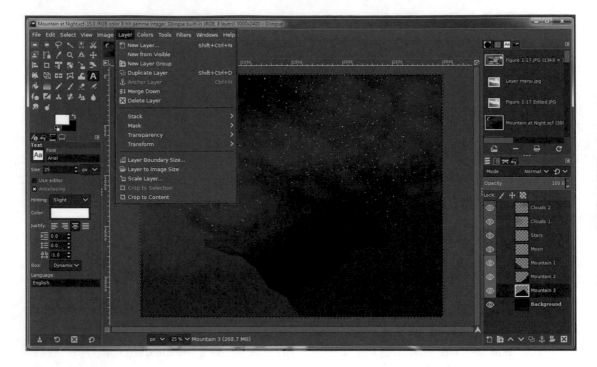

Figure 2-10. *The Layer Menu can be accessed from the Image Menu*

An additional layer menu can also be accessed by right-clicking a layer thumbnail (Figure 2-11). This menu contains options for adjusting the layer's attributes, as well as the options found in the Layers Dialog.

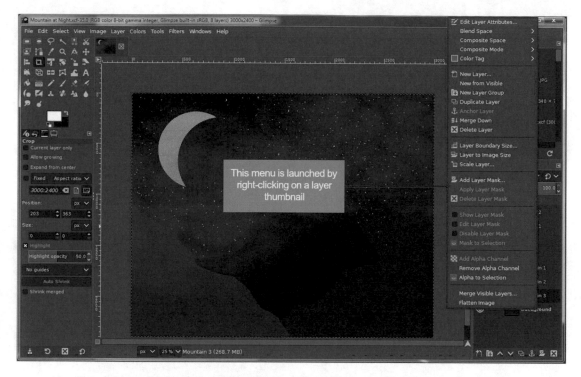

Figure 2-11. *Right-clicking a layer thumbnail launches the Layer Menu*

An Overview of RGB Color Channels

Glimpse opens most images in the RGB color space by default—RGB stands for red, green, and blue, which are the primary colors for this color model. An RGB image is comprised of three *color channels*—one for each color. RGB is an *additive color space*, meaning that colors of each pixel result from combining various amounts of red, green, and blue light. Combining 100% of each results in white, while 0% of each results in black. Figure 2-12 shows a breakdown of each color channel and the composite image.

Figure 2-12. *The red, green, and blue color channels combine to make a composite image*

Layers are constantly used in image editing because they're usually front and center, whereas channels are typically more "behind the scenes." There are times editing a particular color channel may be necessary (typically done by advanced users). Glimpse can decompose an RGB image's channels into layers that display as grayscale images for editing and better viewing of the lightness values of each channel (Figure 2-13).

Figure 2-13. *Channels displayed in grayscale make viewing lightness values easier*

The image can then be recomposed after the editing is complete. You'll have the opportunity to do this in a tutorial coming up in a later chapter.

Alpha channels are related to pixel transparency. An alpha channel is automatically created if there is more than one layer in your image (Figure 2-14).

Figure 2-14. *An alpha channel is automatically created in images with more than one layer*

Selection Masks

Selections are used to isolate part (or multiple parts) of an image. Selections are characterized by a dashed animated boundary line (sometimes called marching ants) around the part of the image being isolated. We'll take a closer look at selections and Selection Tools in Chapter 3.

It may be necessary on occasion to relaunch a selection at a later point in the editing process. For this reason, selections can be saved and stored as channels in the lower section of the Channels Dialog. When a selection is saved to a channel, it is assigned the name *Selection Mask copy* by default (Figure 2-15).

Figure 2-15. *A selection saved to a channel in the lower part of the Channels Dialog*

Note   A Selection Mask is similar to a Layer Mask in the way an overlay can be edited to isolate or protect part of an image. This allows the selection to be modified or refined by using a paintbrush tool on the selection mask. By applying black, white, or gray, the degree of transparency is controlled. A major difference is that rather than being attached to a specific layer, a Selection Mask is stored as a channel.

Selection masks can be refined using the Paintbrush Tool (Figure 2-16). With the visibility toggled on, an overlay becomes visible—the selection edge can be refined by painting with black, white, or gray (for semitransparency).

Figure 2-16.   *The edge refined by using the Paintbrush Tool*

Double-clicking the channel thumbnail preview launches the *Channel Attributes* dialog, in which you can customize the channel's name, assign color tags, adjust the fill opacity, and toggle the switches on or off (Figure 2-17).

Figure 2-17. *Double-clicking the channel's thumbnail preview launches the Channel Attributes Dialog*

The Channels Dialog

As mentioned earlier in this chapter, Glimpse uses the RGB color model by default, which means that the opened color image is composed of red, green, and blue light in various amounts.

There are times (usually, advanced techniques) when editing a specific color channel is necessary, so they can be easily accessed in the Channels Dialog.

At first glance, the Channels Dialog bears a strong resemblance to the Layers Dialog and has similar options, although not quite as many (Figure 2-18).

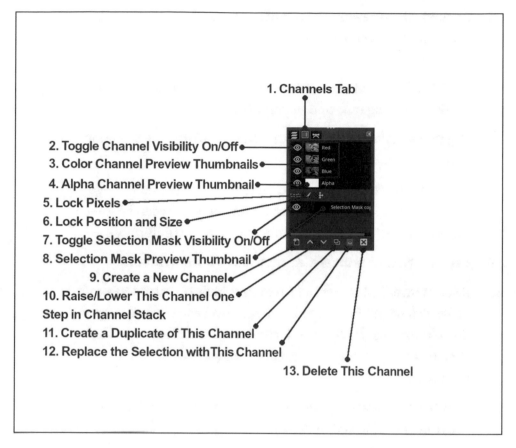

Figure 2-18. *The Channels Dialog*

The Channels Dialog's functions are as follows:

1. **Channels Tab**—Activates the Channels Dialog when clicked.

2. **Toggle Visibility On/Off**—Turns the channel visibility on or off; when toggled off, the image only displays the values of the active channels.

3. **Color Channel Preview Thumbnails**—Displays a small preview image of each color channel.

4. **Alpha Channel Preview Thumbnail**—Displays a small preview image of the alpha channel (like the RGB channels, the visibility can be toggled on/off).

5. **Lock Pixels**—Prevents the use of any brush-based tool on the selection mask's content, protecting it from any unwanted changes.

6. **Lock Position and Size**—When active, prevents the selection mask from being repositioned or resized.

7. **Toggle Selection Mask Visibility On/Off**—Turns the Selection Mask visibility on or off.

8. **Selection Mask Thumbnail**—Displays a small preview image of the Selection Mask (like layers, Selection Masks can be linked together, allowing them to be moved or resized uniformly).

9. **Create a New Channel**—Creates a new Selection Mask.

10. **Raise/Lower This Channel One Level in the Stack**—Moves the active Selection Mask up or down one level each time the up or down arrow is clicked; the Selection Mask can also be moved by clicking and dragging the thumbnail image up or down in the layer stack.

11. **Create a Duplicate of This Channel**—Creates a duplicate of the active channel (selection mask).

12. **Replace the Selection with This Channel**—Adds a selection to the selection mask.

13. **Delete This Channel**—Discards the active selection mask.

An Overview of Paths

Glimpse allows the user to draw complex or irregular shapes by creating *paths using the Paths Tool*. Paths can be used to create illustrations or to make intricate selections (isolating portions of an image).

Figure 2-19 shows the shape of a boxing glove being created. A path is a curved line (sometimes called a Bezier curve) that can be reshaped, stroked (a color, width, or pattern applied), or converted into a selection. Paths are stored in the Paths Dialog—this offers the ability to edit the path at a later date (e.g., if the boxing glove needed to be reshaped). Instead of recreating the boxing glove illustration from scratch, the path could be edited.

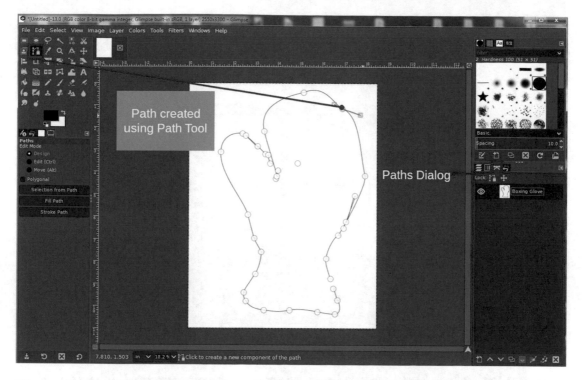

Figure 2-19. *A path is used to create an editable complex or irregular shape*

The path is separate from the image itself, stored away until it's ready to be converted into a selection, or filled/stroked with a color or pattern to create an illustration.

As the path is being drawn, each time the mouse button is clicked, an anchor point is placed (displayed as a small circle) along the path. The path can be reshaped by clicking and dragging a line segment. Clicking in one of the anchor points displays a direction line, allowing you to reshape the portion of the path between two anchor points (Figure 2-20).

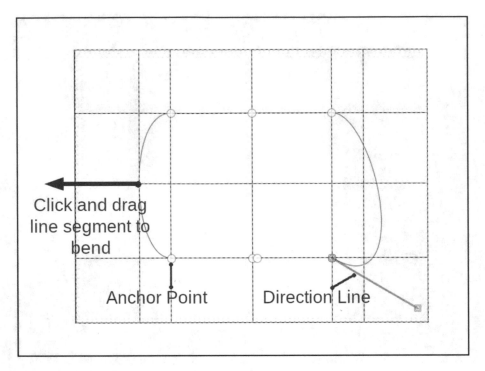

Figure 2-20. *A bend being made in a line segment by clicking and dragging; anchor points and the Direction Line shown*

A selection can be added to a path when needed (Figure 2-21). The path can either be hidden by turning off the visibility or discarded if no longer needed.

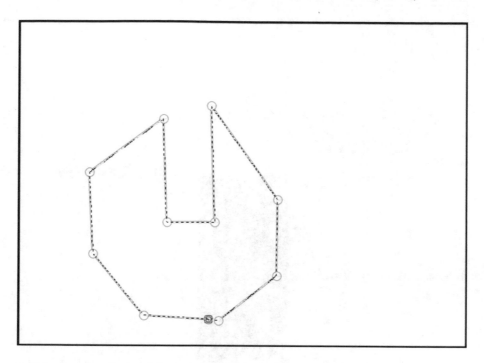

Figure 2-21. *A selection added to a path*

The Paths Dialog

The Paths Dialog looks and functions much like the Layers or Channels Dialogs do (Figure 2-22). This dialog is essential for those who create drawings and work with paths on an ongoing basis.

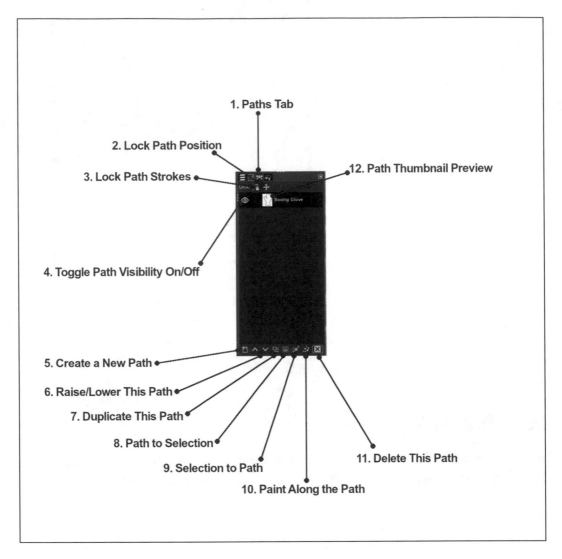

Figure 2-22. *The Paths Dialog looks and functions like the Layers or Channels Dialogs*

The Paths Dialog's functions are as follows:

1. **Paths Tab**—Activates the Paths Dialog when clicked.

2. **Lock Path Position**—Prevents the path from accidental movement.

3. **Lock Path Strokes**—Prevents the path from being reshaped.

4. **Toggle Path Visibility On/Off**—Turns the path's visibility on or off.

5. **Create a New Path**—Enables you to draw a new path independent of others that are already created.

6. **Raise/Lower This Path**—Moves the active path up or down one level each time the up or down arrow is clicked; the path can also be moved by clicking and dragging the thumbnail image up or down in the layer stack.

7. **Duplicate This Path**—Creates a duplicate of the active path.

8. **Path to Selection**—Adds a selection to the active path.

9. **Selection to Path**—Creates a path from an active selection (the visibility will need to be toggled on to see the path).

10. **Paint Along the Path**—Applies a color or pattern to the path.

11. **Delete This Path**—Discards the active path.

12. **Path Thumbnail Preview**—Displays a small preview image of the path (like layers, paths can be linked together, allowing them to be moved or resized uniformly).

An Overview of Undo History

Undo History provides the means to revert to a previous point in your work. To undo one step, you can simply use the keyboard shortcut Ctrl+Z (to redo one step, use Ctrl+Y). However, it may be necessary to undo a series of operations and start over from an earlier point rather than the very beginning.

Caution   If you revert back several operations and then make even a single edit to the image, those steps are gone permanently, and you'll essentially be working from the point that you reverted to. Examine the operations carefully and make sure you don't need them before editing.

The Undo History Dialog

Comparatively speaking, this dialog is the least complex among those covered in this chapter (Figure 2-23).

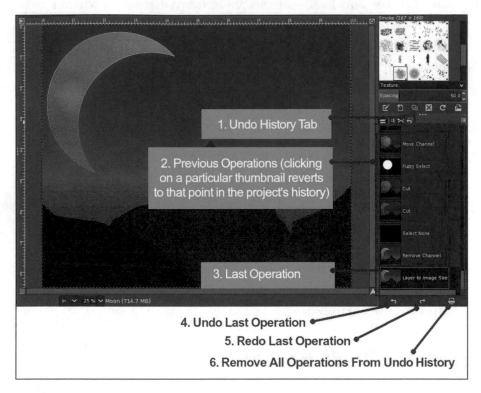

Figure 2-23. *The Undo History Dialog is relatively uncomplicated*

The Undo History Dialog's functions are as follows:

1. **Undo History Tab**—Activates the Undo History Dialog when clicked.

2. **Previous Operations**—Displays "snapshots" of previous operations; clicking a particular thumbnail reverts to that point in history.

3. **Last Operation**—Thumbnail displaying the most recent operation.

4. **Undo Last Operation**—Reverts back one step in history.

5. **Redo Last Operation**—Restores the undone operation.

6. **Remove All Operations from Undo History**—Removes all of the previous operations from the history.

Chapter Conclusion

A lot of ground was covered in this chapter; we looked at layers and the related topics. We then looked at channels—both the color channels and alpha channels that contain selection masks. Next, we looked at paths and how useful they are in drawing complex or irregular shapes. The last item we looked at was Undo History.

In the next chapter, we'll look at the tools used in Glimpse.

CHAPTER 3

An Overview of the Tools

Glimpse offers a large assortment of powerful tools to help you create or edit just about any kind of image. In this chapter, we'll take a look at each tool what it does.

The topics covered in this chapter are

1. An overview of the toolbox, tool options, and tools menu

2. The selection tools

3. The paint tools

4. The transform tools

5. Other tools

The Toolbox, Tool Options, and Tools Menu

In Chapter 1, we briefly glanced at the Toolbox. In this chapter, we'll dive in a little deeper for a closer look. Figure 3-1 shows an overview of the Toolbox and the options available. If you recall, it was mentioned that Glimpse 0.2.0 was updated during the late stages of this book's production. Many of the tool icons in the Toolbox are now nested, meaning they're hidden until the icon is clicked. All of the tools are there, and have the same functionality as the earlier version of Glimpse this book covers. The main difference is that the Toolbox will look smaller with fewer visible tool icons than that shown in the figures throughout this book.

© Phillip Whitt 2020
P. Whitt, *Practical Glimpse*, https://doi.org/10.1007/978-1-4842-6327-3_3

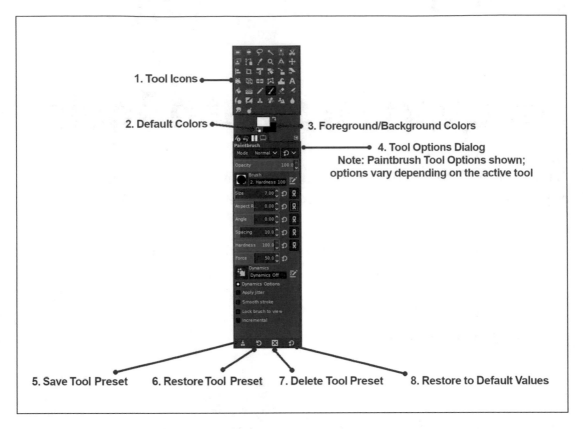

1. Tool Icons

2. Default Colors

3. Foreground/Background Colors

4. Tool Options Dialog
Note: Paintbrush Tool Options shown;
options vary depending on the active tool

5. Save Tool Preset   6. Restore Tool Preset   7. Delete Tool Preset   8. Restore to Default Values

Figure 3-1. *The Toolbox and available options*

Here's a description of what's found in the panel containing toolbox and tool options.

1. **Tool Icons**—A tool is activated by clicking the corresponding icon or using its keyboard shortcut. All but the Perspective Clone and Foreground Select Tools have keyboard shortcuts.

2. **Default Colors**—Clicking this icon (or pressing D on your keyboard) resets the foreground and background colors to their default settings.

3. **Foreground/Background Colors**—Clicking in foreground swatch launches the Change Foreground Color Dialog (or Change Background Color Dialog when clicking the background swatch).

4. **Tool Options Dialog**—This allows the user to change the settings/options of the active tool.

5. **Save Tool Preset**—Saves the current tool settings as a preset, which can be given a custom name.

6. **Restore Tool Preset**—Restores the tool preset to a previous setting, or choose from other presets.

7. **Delete Tool Preset**—Deletes a previously stored preset; most default presets cannot be deleted.

8. **Restore to Default Values**—Resets the current tool settings to the original settings.

Tool Options

The Tool Options Menu is where the user can change the tool settings to suit the task at hand. Most tools offer numerous options—Figure 3-2 shows the options available for the Rectangle Select Tool.

Figure 3-2. *The tool settings available for the Rectangle Select Tool*

Tools Menu

The Tools Menu is accessed from the Image Menu—this is simply just another place in Glimpse to access the tools. It opens the Tools Menu, and clicking a specific tool category opens submenu; clicking a single tool (such as Paths or Text) makes that tool active. Figure 3-3 shows the Tools menu opened from the Image Menu.

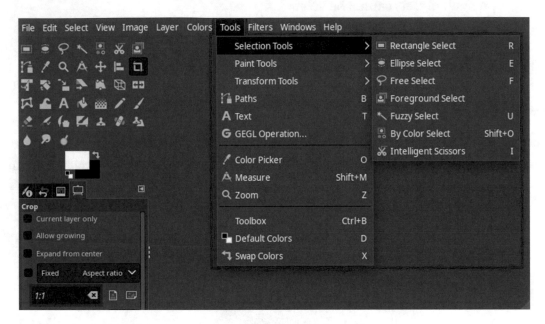

Figure 3-3. *The Tools Menu accessed from the Image Menu*

The Selection Tools

The Selection Tools allow the user to isolate portions of the image. They can also be used to create shapes that can be filled with colors or patterns. There are a wide variety of selection tools in Glimpse that function in different ways—for example, some work by clicking and dragging around the area to be isolated, others work by selecting an area of a specific color range.

In the example shown in Figure 3-4, two different tools (that function in different ways) are being used to select the flower—the Fuzzy Select Tool, which selects a contiguous area based on color (in this case, the tool was used to select the solid light background, then the selection was inverted), and the Scissors Select Tool, which detects the edge between areas of contrast.

Figure 3-4. *A comparison of two different tools being used to select an object*

The selection can be adjusted from the Tool Options Menu. One example is that a selection can be either hard-edged or feathered (feathering creates a soft, transitional edge). Figure 3-5 shows an example of rectangular shapes created by filling in a hard-edged selection with a solid color, then filling in a feathered selection with that same color.

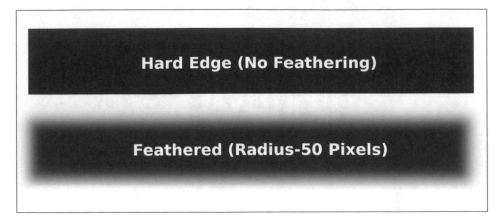

Figure 3-5. *A comparison of shapes created from filling a hard selection and a feathered selection*

Selections have other options available (Figure 3-6), and they vary depending on the type of selection tool being used.

Selections have four *modes* available:

1. Replace the current selection

2. Add to the current selection (Shift)

3. Subtract from the current selection (Ctrl)

4. Intersect with the current selection (Shift+Ctrl)

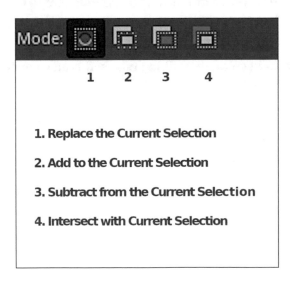

Figure 3-6. *The Selection Modes*

Glimpse offers seven selection tools, shown listed in Table 3-1—this provides a brief overview of each tool and its function.

Table 3-1. *The selection tools available in Glimpse*

Tool	Keyboard Shortcut	Tool Description
Rectangle Select	R	Selects rectangular or square regions
Ellipse Select	E	Selects elliptical or circular regions
Free Select	F	Selects hand-drawn free or polygonal irregularly shaped regions
Fuzzy Select	U	Selects a contiguous region based on color
Select by Color	Shift+O	Selects regions with similar colors
Scissors Select	I	Selects by detecting the edge between areas of contrast
Foreground Select	No shortcut	Selects a region containing foreground objects

The Paint Tools

The paint tools are used to apply colors and patterns, and in some instances are used to alter or change tonal quality. Some work like conventional painting tools, and others function a bit differently.

Figure 3-7 shows an example of stroke created using the Paintbrush Tool (holding the Shift key creates a straight line). These are examples of a hard brush tip compared to a soft brush tip.

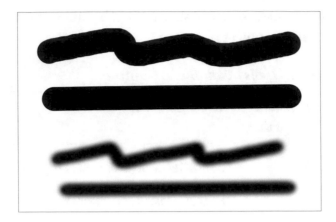

Figure 3-7. *A comparison of hard and soft brush tips*

There are a variety of brush tips available to mimic different types of media, such as chalk, acrylic, and so on. Figure 3-8 shows the various brush tip styles.

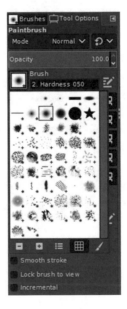

Figure 3-8. *The various brush tips available in Glimpse*

Two brush tools that are very useful in photo retouching and restoration are the Clone and Healing Tools. The Clone Tool essentially copies pixels from one part of the image and then pastes them onto another. It's useful for covering unwanted areas of an image by "borrowing" from another part of the image.

The Healing Tool is similar to the Clone Tool, but instead of pasting an exact copy of the sampled area, it blends in color, tone, and texture from the surrounding area to make a calculated repair. This tool is very useful for retouching portraits and used in removing blemishes and other flaws. Figure 3-9 shows a comparison of the two tools.

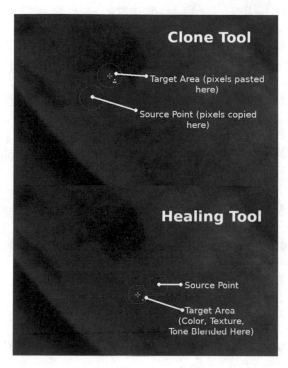

Figure 3-9. *The Clone Tool and the Healing Tool*

Glimpse offers a large selection of paint tools, shown listed in Table 3-2—this provides a brief overview of each tool and its function.

Table 3-2. *The paint tools available in Glimpse*

Tool	Keyboard Shortcut	Tool Description
Bucket Fill	Shift+B	Fills selected areas with color or a pattern
Gradient	G	Fills a selected area with a color gradient (a gradual transition from one color to another)
Pencil	N	Creates hard-edged strokes similar to that of a conventional pencil
Paintbrush	P	Creates smooth strokes similar to that of a conventional paintbrush
Eraser	Shift+E	Erases (removes) pixels to the background or transparency
Airbrush	A	Creates paint strokes with variable pressure
Ink	K	Creates calligraphy-style strokes
MyPaint Brush	Y	Uses MyPaint brushes in Glimpse
Clone	C	Copies pixels from one area and pastes them to another area
Healing	H	Corrects defects such as blemishes or image irregularities
Perspective Clone	No shortcut	Clones from an image source after applying a perspective transformation
Blur/Sharpen	Shift+U	Applies selective blurring or sharpening using a brush
Smudge	S	Applies selective smudging using a brush
Dodge/Burn	Shift+D	Selectively lightens or darkens using a brush

The Transform Tools

The transform tools in Glimpse are used to move, reshape, rotate, or otherwise transform layers, selections, or paths. The Crop Tool is a commonly used transform tool (found in virtually any image editing program)—it transforms the image by trimming away unwanted edges (Figure 3-10).

Figure 3-10. *The Crop Tool is one of the most essential transform tools*

Another example of a useful transform tool is the *Unified Transform Tool.* It's used to rotate, scale (resize), shear, and modify perspective. In Figure 3-11, it's being used to correct the perspective of a church that has a slant to it in the image.

Figure 3-11. *The Unified Transform Tool combines several transform tools into one*

Glimpse offers a large selection of transform tools, shown listed in Table 3-3—this provides a brief overview of each tool and its function.

Table 3-3. *The transform tools available in Glimpse*

Tool	Keyboard Shortcut	Tool Description
Align	Q	Aligns or arranges layers and other objects
Move	M	Moves layers, selections, and other objects
Crop	Shift+C	Removes edges to trim images
Rotate	Shift+R	Rotates the layer, selection, or path
Scale	Shift+S	Scales (resizes) the layer, selection, or path
Shear	Shift+H	Shears (slants) the layer, selection, or path
Perspective	Shift+P	Changes the perspective of the layer, selection, or path
United Transform	Shift+T	This combines the Rotate, Scale, Shear, and Perspective functions in one tool
Handle Transform	Shift+L	Deforms the layer, selection, or path with handles
Flip	Shift+F	Reverses the layer, selection, or path horizontally or vertically
Cage Transform	Shift+G	Deforms a selection with a cage-type boundary
Deform Transform	W	Deforms using different tools

Other Tools

The other tools not assigned to a specific category provide several miscellaneous functions. One example is the Text Tool which creates a text layer for adding text to the image. The text color, size, and font (typeface) can be changed to suit the task (Figure 3-12).

Figure 3-12. *The Text Tool is used for adding text to an image*

The Color Picker Tool is another useful item—it can be used to set the foreground color as shown in Figure 3-13. It can also be used to set the background color, add a color to the palette, pick only, or display the Info Window (this shows the mixture of RGB light composing the color).

Figure 3-13. *The Color Picker Tool can be used to set the foreground color, among other functions*

Glimpse offers several of these "miscellaneous" tools, shown listed in Table 3-4—this provides a brief overview of each tool and its function.

Table 3-4. *The other tools available in Glimpse*

Tool	Keyboard Shortcut	Tool Description
Paths	B	Creates and edits paths
Text	T	Creates or edits text layers
Color Picker	O	Sets colors from the image pixels
Measure	Shift+M	Measures distances and angles between objects
Zoom	Z	Adjusts the zoom level
Default Colors/Swap Colors	D (default), X (swap)	Sets the foreground and background colors to their default settings; swaps the foreground and background colors
GEGL operation (not shown in the Toolbox)	No keyboard shortcut	Applies a GEGL operation

Chapter Conclusion

As we can see, there are many tools available in Glimpse. There's a tool for just about any task.

Here's what was covered in this chapter:

An overview of the toolbox, tool options, and tools menu

The selection tools

The paint tools

The transform tools

Other tools

In the next chapter, we'll dive into some actual work by learning about making tonal and exposure corrections.

PART II

Working with Digital Photos

CHAPTER 4

Correcting Exposure and Contrast

In this chapter, we'll get to do some actual editing...finally! Glimpse is a great program for correcting problem areas such as exposure, contrast, and other tonal issues.

Note The first few methods of making tonal corrections are fairly simple. They can be useful for making quick corrections (especially for beginners desiring to gain a little experience and confidence). The last part of the chapter introduces the most powerful tonal correction tools (Levels and Curves)—they take more time to master, but it's time well invested.

The topics covered in this chapter are

Tutorial 1: Using the Exposure dialog

Tutorial 2: Lightening dark areas using the Shadows-Highlights dialog

Tutorial 3: Improving contrast using the Brightness-Contrast dialog

The Levels dialog

Understanding the histogram

Tutorial 4: Improving contrast using Levels

The Curves dialog

Tutorial 5: Improving local tonality using Curves

Chapter conclusion

© Phillip Whitt 2020
P. Whitt, *Practical Glimpse*, https://doi.org/10.1007/978-1-4842-6327-3_4

Note   Most digital photos (particularly scanned film-based photographs) can benefit from corrective sharpening. In most of the tutorials throughout this book, we'll use the *Unsharp Mask* filter as the last step. Basically, this filter improves the apparent sharpness of the image by increasing contrast in the edges of the elements in the image. For a detailed description of the Unsharp Mask filter, click here: `https://docs.gimp.org/2.6/en/plug-in-unsharp-mask.html`.

Tutorial 1: Using the Exposure Dialog

In this lesson, the *Exposure* dialog will be used to brighten an old photograph that was underexposed when it was shot (which means the light levels were too low when the film was exposed). Using the Exposure dialog mimics increased light levels by increasing the brightness of every pixel in the image.

1. Open the practice image *Ch_4_Dark_Boat* in Glimpse.

2. Create a duplicate of the background layer (Right-Click ➤ Duplicate Layer) and rename it (*Work Layer*, or something similar).

3. Launch the Exposure dialog (Colors ➤ Exposure)—by ticking the *Split view* option, a side-by-side view comparing the effect applied shown against the original is displayed.

4. Set the Exposure value to about 2.25 (Figure 4-1)—do not click the OK button just yet.

Figure 4-1. *Setting the Exposure value with the Split view option enabled*

5. This action caused the areas that are supposed to be dark to become muddy, so now we'll offset this by adjusting the Black level. Set the Black level value to 0.002, then click OK (Figure 4-2).

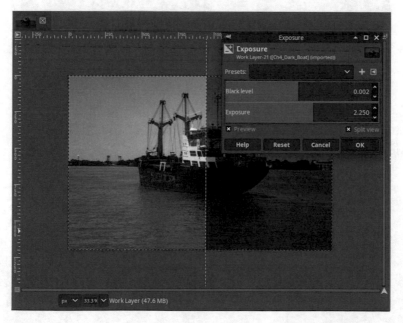

Figure 4-2. *Setting the Black level value darkens the shadow areas that became muddy*

6. The last thing to do is to slightly sharpen the image. Open the Unsharp Mask dialog (Filters ➤ Enhance ➤ Sharpen (Unsharp Mask)).

7. Set the Radius to 1.00, leaving Amount and Threshold at their default settings (Figure 4-3), then click OK.

Figure 4-3. *Setting the Radius in the Unsharp Mask dialog*

Figure 4-4 shows the before and after comparison. When done, you can save as an .XCF file if you want to keep the file, or simply close it out.

Figure 4-4. *The before and after comparison*

Overview of the Shadows-Highlights Dialog

Shadows-Highlights is a bit more complex than most of the other dialogs in Glimpse. It's used to control exposure in shadow and highlight areas in an image, allowing for precise control (Figure 4-5).

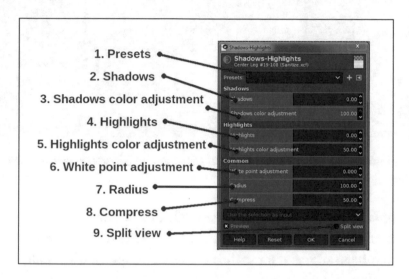

Figure 4-5. *The Shadows-Highlights dialog*

The Shadows-Highlights dialog's functions are as follows:

1. **Presets**—Allows the user to save the current value settings; this is useful when reapplying the same adjustments to multiple images, eliminating the need to manually adjust the settings each time.

2. **Shadows**—Adjusts the exposure in the shadow (darkest) areas of the image.

3. **Shadows Color Adjustment**—Adjusts the color saturation in the shadow (darkest) areas of the image.

4. **Highlights**—Adjusts the exposure in the highlight (lightest) areas of the image.

5. **Highlights Color Adjustment**—Adjusts the color saturation in the highlight (lightest) areas of the image.

6. **White Point Adjustment**—Shifts the white point of the image.

7. **Radius**—Spatial extent (essentially expands or narrows range of effect). Figure 4-6 shows an example of the shadows being lightened, and the radius expanding the range a bit further (note the shadows cast on the ground).

Shadow Slider set to 75.00

Shadow Slider set to 75.00
Radius Slider set to 35.00

Figure 4-6. *A comparison of the original image, the Shadow slider, and the Radius slider*

8. **Compress**—Compresses the effect while preserving midtones. Normally, the subject in the photograph is in the midtone range and has been adjusted for in the camera's settings, so it's usually desirable to preserve these.

9. **Split View**—Provides a side-by-side view of the image with and without effect applied.

Tutorial 2: Lightening Dark Areas Using the Shadows-Highlights Dialog

In this lesson, the *Shadows-Highlights* dialog will be used to lighten a portion of a digital photograph that is underexposed while preserving the midtones and highlights.

1. Open the practice image *Ch4_Dark Foreground* in Glimpse.

2. Create a duplicate of the background layer (Right-Click ➤ Duplicate Layer) and rename it (*Work Layer*, or something similar).

3. Launch the Shadows-Highlights dialog (Colors ➤ Shadows-Highlights)—by ticking the *Split view* option, a side-by-side view comparing the effect applied shown against the original is displayed.

4. Set the *Shadows* slider to 60.00-65.00, the White point adjustment
    to 2.00, and the *Radius* slider to 10.00; click OK when done
    (Figure 4-7).

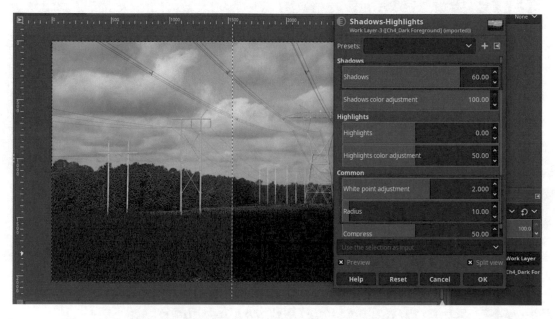

Figure 4-7. *Set the Shadows slider to 60.00–65.00, the White point adjustment to 2.00, and the Radius slider to 10.00, then click OK*

5. The last thing to do is to slightly sharpen the image. Open the
    Unsharp Mask dialog (Filters ➤ Enhance ➤ Sharpen (Unsharp
    Mask)).

6. Set the Radius to 1.00, leaving Amount and Threshold at their
    default settings (Figure 4-8), then click OK.

Note   I zoomed in a great deal to show the subtle but noticeable difference that
the Unsharp Mask filter made.

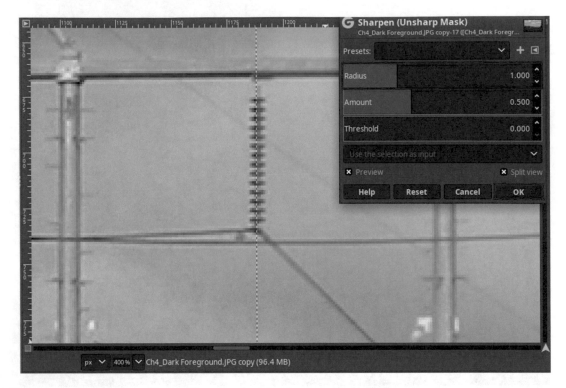

Figure 4-8. *Setting the Radius in the Unsharp Mask dialog*

Figure 4-9 shows the before and after comparison. When done, you can save as an .XCF file if you want to keep the file, or simply close it out.

Figure 4-9. *The before and after comparison*

Tutorial 3: Improving Contrast Using the Brightness-Contrast Dialog

In this tutorial, we'll call on the easy-to-use Brightness-Contrast dialog. It can be a useful dialog, but it's a bit limited compared to other tonal adjustment dialogs (such as Levels or Curves).

It's a useful feature for making minor global (overall) tonal corrections in dull images. But more often than not, it lacks the precision to make a correction without overdoing the result. Figure 4-10 shows how easy it is to blow out the highlights and lose detail.

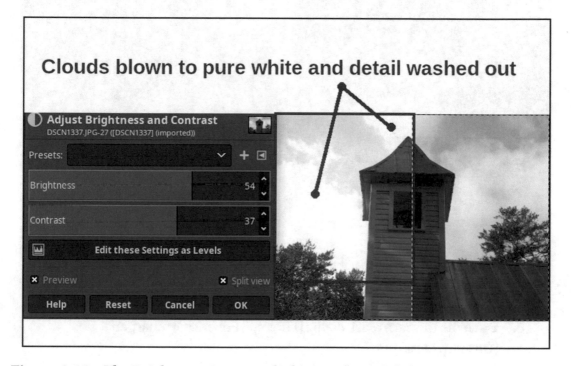

Figure 4-10. *The Brightness-Contrast dialog can "overdo" the result, such as blowing out highlights*

Now we'll use the Brightness-Contrast dialog to improve an old photo that has dull contrast.

1. Open the practice image *Ch4_Baby_in_Bath* in Glimpse.

2. Create a duplicate of the background layer (Right-Click ➤ Duplicate Layer) and rename it (*Work Layer*, or something similar).

3. Open the Brightness-Contrast dialog (Colors ➤ Brightness-Contrast).

4. Set the Contrast slider to 53; click OK when done (Figure 4-11).

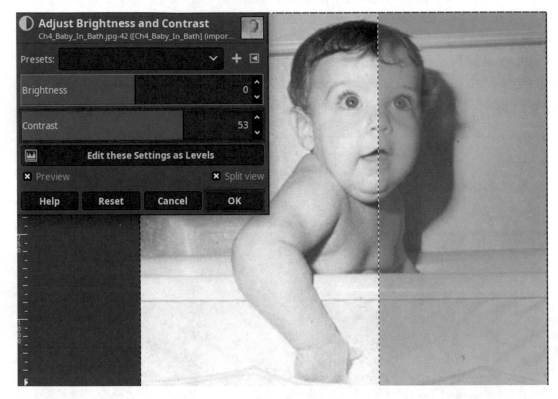

Figure 4-11. *Set the Contrast slider to 53 to boost the contrast in this dull image*

5. Open the Unsharp Mask dialog (Filters ➤ Enhance ➤ Sharpen (Unsharp Mask)).

6. Because this is an old image, we'll sharpen it a bit more than the previous ones. Leave at the default settings (Radius 3.0, Amount 0.50, and Threshold 0.0), then click OK (Figure 4-12).

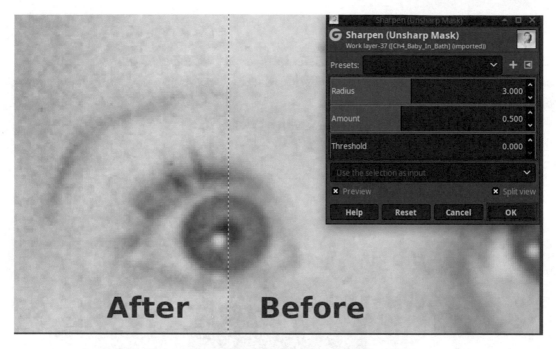

Figure 4-12. *Leave the Unsharp Mask dialog at the default settings*

Figure 4-13 shows the before and after comparison. When done, you can save as an .XCF file if you want to keep the file, or simply close it out.

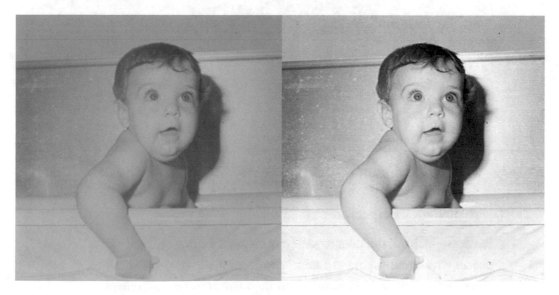

Figure 4-13. *The before and after comparison*

The Levels Dialog

The *Levels* dialog is an extremely useful feature. Levels can be used to make tonal corrections, such as making an image lighter, darker, or boosting the contrast with great precision.

Figure 4-14 shows the Levels dialog, with a brief description on most of the functions.

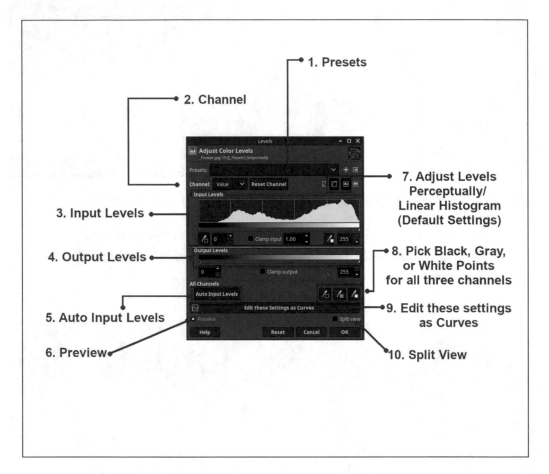

Figure 4-14. *The Levels dialog*

The Levels dialog's functions are as follows:

1. **Presets**—Allows the user to save the current value settings; this is useful when reapplying the same adjustments to multiple images, eliminating the need to manually adjust the settings each time.

2. **Channel**—Adjusts the composite channel, or the red, green, and blue channels individually.

3. **Input Levels**—The tonal information is essentially "remapped" by using the black, midtone, or white sliders. The numeric input boxes can also be used. The eye drop icons are used to pick black or white points for the selected channel (composite or the red, green, or blue channel).

4. **Output Levels**—Allows the output level range to be limited or constrained; an example would be moving the white slider to the left set a lower maximum value for the highlights.

5. **Auto Input Levels**—Automatically adjusts levels for all channels.

6. **Preview**—When this box is checked, the effect is shown in real time as the adjustments are being made.

7. **Adjust Levels Perceptually/Linear Histogram**—These are the default levels adjustment and histogram readout settings.

8. **Pick Black, Gray, or White Points for All Channels**—Makes tonal adjustments in the composite channel.

9. **Edit These Settings As Curves**—Instantly switches from Levels to the Curves dialog.

10. **Split View**—A side-by-side view comparing the effect applied shown against the original is displayed.

Understanding the Histogram

The Levels dialog displays a *histogram*, which is a graphical representation of the pixel brightness values ranging from 0 (100% black) to 255 (100% white).

Figure 4-15 shows a black-and-white (grayscale, to be technically correct) image with the Levels dialog open. The tonal information of the image of the car is mapped in the histogram. The darkest pixels are in the left portion of the histogram, the middle-range pixels in the center portion, and the lightest pixels in the right portion.

Figure 4-15. *The tonal information of this image is mapped in the histogram*

If you'll notice, most of the data spans most of the length of the histogram with no large gaps.

However, in Figure 4-16, we can see there is a gap in the shadows portion, and an even larger gap in the highlights portion. The image is dull, a bit dark, and lacking contrast—the lack of highlight values is the main reason.

Figure 4-16. *There are gaps in the shadow and highlight portions of the histogram*

Tutorial 4: Improving Contrast Using Levels

Now we'll use the Levels dialog to improve the contrast of the same image that the Brightness-Contrast dialog was used on.

1. Open the practice image *Ch4_Baby_in_Bath* in Glimpse.

2. Create a duplicate of the background layer (Right-Click ➤ Duplicate Layer) and rename it (*Work Layer*, or something similar).

3. Open the Levels dialog (Colors ➤ Levels).

4. Now, we'll make the following adjustments (Figure 4-17):

    - Move the black slider (input levels) to the right until the value is 76.

    - Move the white slider (input levels) to the left until the value is 195.

    - Click OK when done.

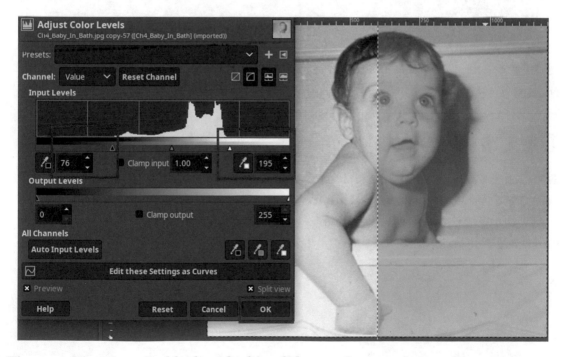

Figure 4-17. *Move the black and white sliders as shown to bring out contrast*

5. As we did in the previous tutorial, we'll sharpen the image a bit. Launch the Unsharp Mask filter dialog (Filters ➤ Enhance ➤ Sharpen (Unsharp Mask)).

6. Leave at the default settings (Radius 3.0, Amount 0.50, and Threshold 0.0), then click OK.

Figure 4-18 shows the before and after comparison. When done, you can save as an .XCF file if you want to keep the file, or simply close it out.

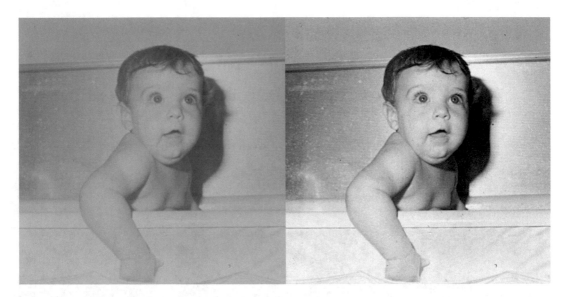

Figure 4-18. *The before and after comparison*

The Curves Dialog

The *Curves* dialog is another useful feature—like levels, curves can be used to make tonal corrections and color corrections, but it offers greater precision.

Figure 4-19 shows the Curves dialog, with a brief description on most of the key functions.

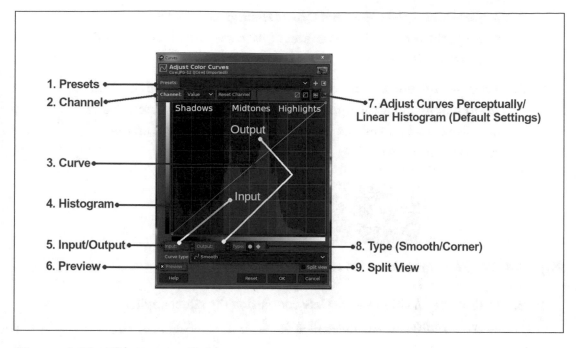

Figure 4-19. *The Curves dialog*

The Curves dialog's functions are as follows:

1. **Presets**—Allows the user to save the current value settings; this is useful when reapplying the same adjustments to multiple images, eliminating the need to manually adjust the settings each time.

2. **Channel**—Adjusts the composite channel, or the red, green, and blue channels individually.

3. **Curve**—This line can be curved to make adjustments in tone or color.

4. **Histogram**—Graphical display of the pixel brightness.

5. **Input/Output**—Displays the x/y position of the cursor on the grid as the curve is being adjusted.

6. **Preview**—When this box is checked, the effect is shown in real time as the adjustments are being made.

7. **Adjust Curves Perceptually/Linear Histogram**—Default settings; the other two settings are *Adjust curves in linear light* and *Logarithmic histogram.*

8. *Type*—Configure as a curve or angled; the *Curve type* option offers smooth or freehand; an option of a curve with rounded arcs, or a pencil-like tool that allows the user to draw sharp angles on the curve (Figure 4-20).

Figure 4-20. *The Smooth and Freehand curve types*

9. **Split View**—A side-by-side view comparing the effect applied shown against the original is displayed.

The example in Figure 4-21 shows a comparison of the *Smooth* and *Corner* settings. Depending on the adjustment being made, one setting may be better suited than the other. For example, the Smooth setting produces a more gradual effect (and, in most cases, is probably the most useful setting), and the Corner setting produces slightly different tonal changes.

Figure 4-21. *A comparison of the Smooth and Corner curve settings*

The example in Figure 4-22 shows an example of an *"S" curve*. The center of the line is anchored while a slight s-shape is made to improve dull contrast. The center of the line represents the areas in the image that are mainly average in luma and tone; an anchor point is placed by clicking the line.

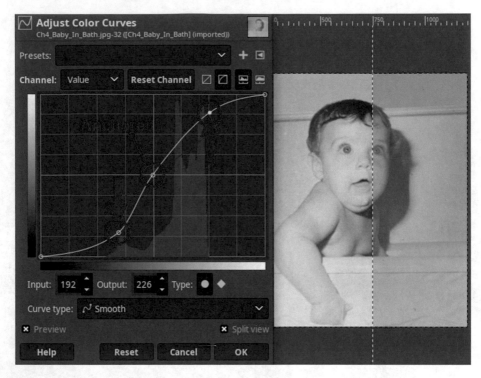

Figure 4-22. *An example of an "S" curve, which is used to improve contrast*

Tutorial 5: Improving Local Tonality Using Curves

Now we'll use the Curves dialog to reduce the harshness in the shadows of a slightly underexposed image. This adjustment localizes the darkest areas and lightens them slightly while leaving the midtones and highlights mostly unaffected.

1. Open the practice image *Ch4_Lighten_Shadows* in Glimpse.

2. Create a duplicate of the background layer (Right-Click ➤ Duplicate Layer) and rename it (*Work Layer*, or something similar).

3. Open the Curves dialog (Colors ➤ Curves).

4. We'll make a slight bend in the curve to lighten the shadows. As shown in Figure 4-23, place an anchor point on the grid (input: 160/output: 160), and bend the curve slightly upward (input: 64/ output 160).

Figure 4-23. *Adjust the curve as shown to lighten the shadows*

5. Now, we'll sharpen the image a bit. Launch the Unsharp Mask filter dialog (Filters ➤ Enhance ➤ Sharpen (Unsharp Mask)).

6. Set the Radius to 1.00, leaving Amount and Threshold at their default settings (Figure 4-24), then click OK.

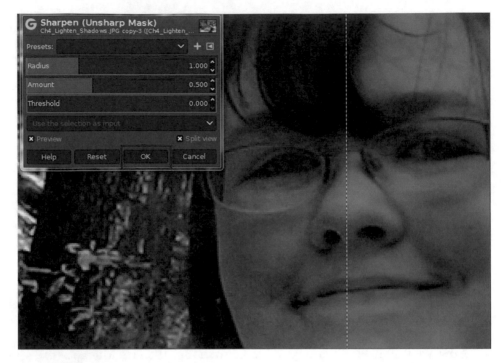

Figure 4-24. *Setting the Radius in the Unsharp Mask dialog*

Figure 4-25 shows the before and after comparison. The effect is just enough to lighten the shadows a little. When done, you can save as an .XCF file if you want to keep the file, or simply close it out.

Figure 4-25. *The before and after comparison*

Chapter Conclusion

This chapter provided several tutorials on correcting tonal problems (such as exposure and contrast).

Here are the main topics that were covered:

- Using the Exposure dialog

- Lightening dark areas using the Shadows-Highlights dialog

- Improving contrast using the Brightness-Contrast dialog

- The Levels dialog

- Understanding the histogram

- Improving contrast using Levels

- The Curves dialog

- Improving local tonality using Curves

In the next chapter, we'll look at working with color and making color corrections.

CHAPTER 5

Enhancing, Correcting, and Working with Color

In this chapter, we'll now learn about improving color images—both enhancing color and correcting color problems. We'll also work with color by colorizing a grayscale (black-and-white image).

The topics covered in this chapter are

Tutorial 6: Correcting an unwanted color cast using Color Balance

The Color Temperature dialog

Tutorial 7: Correcting an image using Color Temperature

Tutorial 8: Restoring faded color using Levels

Tutorial 9: Restoring faded color using Auto White Balance

Tutorial 10: Turning a color image to sepia using Desaturate

Tutorial 11: Turning a color image to black and white using Mono Mixer

Tutorial 12: Colorizing a black-and-white photo

Chapter conclusion

Tutorial 6: Correcting a Color Shift Using Color Balance

The *Color Balance* dialog is often used to correct images with color casts—essentially, this means shifting from the excess of a specific color by offsetting it with its opposite (complementary color) to rebalance the image. Figure 5-1 shows the Color Balance

© Phillip Whitt 2020
P. Whitt, *Practical Glimpse*, https://doi.org/10.1007/978-1-4842-6327-3_5

dialog's complementary color pairs—the more one color is increased, the more its opposite is subtracted (e.g., increasing red reduces cyan and vice versa).

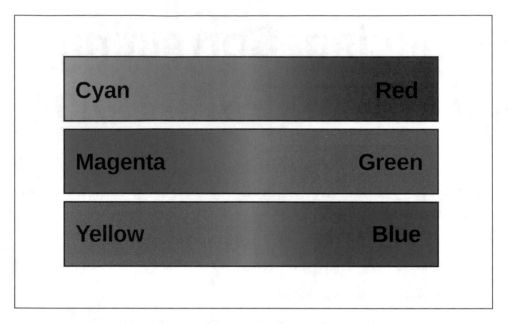

Figure 5-1. *The color pairs used by the Color Balance dialog*

In this case, we'll correct an image with a blue color cast by offsetting it using yellow (blue's opposite). We'll make separate adjustments in the shadows and the midtones.

Note   Not all color casts are necessarily undesirable. For example, taking a photograph in the evening before sunset may produce a golden or yellow color cast that lends an ideal mood for the image. Undesirable color casts are often a result of chemical changes in the photographic print over the years, or the camera's settings (such as white balance) being improperly set.

---

1. Open the practice image *Ch5_Blue_Color_Cast* in Glimpse.

2. Create a duplicate of the background layer (Right-Click ➤ Duplicate Layer) and rename it (*Work Layer,* or something similar).

3. Launch the Color Balance dialog (Colors ➤ Color Balance)—by ticking the *Split view* option, a side-by-side view comparing the effect applied shown against the original is displayed.

4. As shown in Figure 5-2, make the following adjustments:

    - Click the Shadows button.

    - Deselect the Preserve Luminosity option (the X in the box will not appear).

    - Move the Yellow-Blue slider to the left until the value is −40.00 (or double-click in the slider and enter the new values using the keyboard).

    - Do not click OK yet.

Figure 5-2. Adjusting the Shadows Range in the Color Balance dialog

5. Now, we'll make some adjustments in the midtone range (Figure 5-3).

    - Click the Midtones button.

    - Leave the Preserve Luminosity option deselected (the X in the box will not appear).

- Move the Yellow-Blue slider to the left until the value is –25.00 (or double-click in the slider and enter the new values using the keyboard).

- Click OK.

Figure 5-3. *Adjusting the Midtones Range in the Color Balance dialog*

6. The last thing to do is to slightly sharpen the image. Open the Unsharp Mask dialog (Filters ➤ Enhance ➤ Sharpen (Unsharp Mask)).

7. Set the Radius to 1.00, leaving Amount and Threshold at their default settings (Figure 5-4), then click OK.

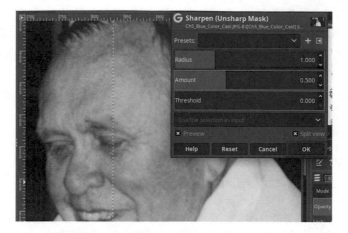

Figure 5-4. *Setting the Radius in the Unsharp Mask dialog*

Figure 5-5 shows the before and after comparison. When done, you can save as an .XCF file if you want to keep the file, or simply close it out.

Figure 5-5. *The before and after comparison*

Tutorial 7: Correcting an Image Using Color Temperature

In this lesson, we'll use the *Color Temperature* dialog to warm an image that has a cool color temperature that happened as a result of the camera's white balance setting being improperly set.

Note   Measured in Kelvin, color temperature refers how warm or cool the lighting in an image is. In this tutorial, the image is warmed by increasing the temperature from 6500 to 11000.

1. Open the practice image *Ch5_Cool_Temp* in Glimpse.

2. Create a duplicate of the background layer (Right-Click ➤ Duplicate Layer) and rename it (*Work Layer,* or something similar).

3. Launch the Color Temperature dialog (Colors ➤ Color Temperature)—by ticking the *Split view* option, a side-by-side view comparing the effect applied shown against the original is displayed.

4. Set the *Intended Temperature* slider to 11000, and click OK when done (Figure 5-6). This gives the image a noticeably warmer look, correcting the image.

Figure 5-6. *Set the Intended Temperature to 11000*

5. The last thing to do is to slightly sharpen the image. Open the Unsharp Mask dialog (Filters ➤ Enhance ➤ Sharpen (Unsharp Mask)).

6. Set the Radius to 1.00, leaving Amount and Threshold at their
    default settings (Figure 5-7), then click OK.

Note   I zoomed in a great deal to show the subtle but noticeable difference that
the Unsharp Mask filter made.

Figure 5-7. *Setting the Radius in the Unsharp Mask dialog*

Figure 5-8 shows the before and after comparison. When done,
you can save as an .XCF file if you want to keep the file, or simply
close it out.

Figure 5-8. *The before and after comparison*

The Color Temperature dialog also contains a selection of preset temperatures as shown in Figure 5-9.

Figure 5-9. *The Color Temperature dialog presets*

Tutorial 8: Restoring Faded Colors Using Levels

In the last chapter, we used Levels to improve the contrast of a dull black-and-white image.

In this tutorial, we'll use Levels to remap the tonal information of each color channel to restore a faded color photo.

1. Open the practice image *Ch5_Faded_Color* in Glimpse.

2. Create a duplicate of the background layer (Right-Click ➤ Duplicate Layer) and rename it (*Work Layer*, or something similar).

3. Open the Levels dialog (Colors ➤ Levels).

4. Under the Channel setting, select Red—move the black slider to the right the numeric value is 68, then move the white slider to the left until the numeric value is 206 (Figure 5-10). *Do not* press the OK button yet.

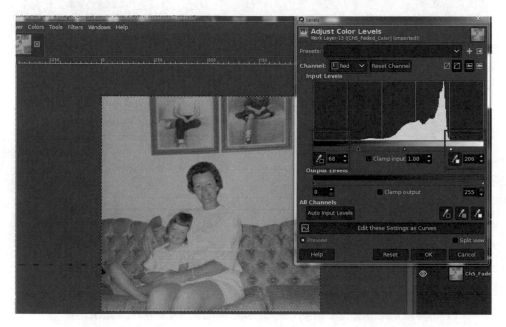

Figure 5-10. *Adjusting the Red Channel in Levels to the settings shown*

5. Under the Channel setting, select Green—move the black slider to the right the numeric value is 58, then move the white slider to the left until the numeric value is 200 (Figure 5-11). *Do not* press the OK button yet.

Figure 5-11. *Adjusting the Green Channel in Levels to the settings shown*

6. Under the Channel setting, select Blue—move the black slider to
    the right the numeric value is 45, then move the white slider to
    the left until the numeric value is 175 (Figure 5-12). Press the OK
    button when finished.

Figure 5-12. *Adjusting the Blue Channel in Levels to the settings shown*

7. We can see the image looks much better, but it could stand a bit of sharpening. Open the Unsharp Mask dialog (Filters ➤ Enhance ➤ Sharpen (Unsharp Mask)).

8. Set the Radius to 2.00, leaving Amount and Threshold at their default settings (Figure 5-13), then click OK.

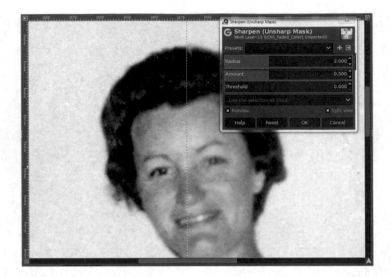

Figure 5-13. *Setting the Radius to 2.00 in the Unsharp Mask dialog*

Figure 5-14 shows the before and after comparison. When done, you can save as an .XCF file if you want to keep the file, or simply close it out.

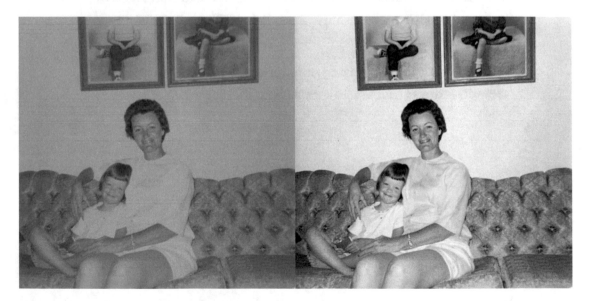

Figure 5-14. *The before and after comparison*

Tutorial 9: Restoring Color Using Auto White Balance

If you're processing a large batch of old photographs (such as old family photos), using *Auto White Balance* can be a time-saver, although the results may be hit or miss. The results may be satisfactory, but not perfect.

In this tutorial, we'll use Auto White Balance to restore an old photo that not only has faded colors but color shifts (meaning the dyes in the photo have shifted from the original colors over time). In the process, the contrast will also be improved.

1. Open the practice image *Ch5_White_Balance* in Glimpse.

2. Create a duplicate of the background layer (Right-Click ➤ Duplicate Layer) and rename it (*Work Layer*, or something similar).

3. Initiate the Auto White Balance command as seen in Figure 5-15 (Colors ➤ Auto ➤ White Balance).

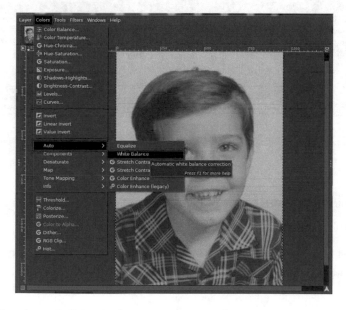

Figure 5-15. *The Auto White Balance command*

4. There's an immediate improvement; the colors look much more natural and the contrast improved. However, there's a loss of density that results from years of degradation, so we'll restore some of it.

5. Create a duplicate of the Work Layer (Right-Click ➤ Duplicate Layer).

6. Change the Blend Mode from Normal to Multiply, then lower the layer's opacity from to 35–40% (Figure 5-16).

Figure 5-16. *Changing the Blend Mode to Multiply restores some of the lost density*

7. Right-click the Work Layer Copy thumbnail, then select Merge Down.

8. The last thing to do is to slightly sharpen the image. Open the Unsharp Mask dialog (Filters ➤ Enhance ➤ Sharpen (Unsharp Mask)).

9. Set the Radius to 1.00, leaving Amount and Threshold at their default settings (Figure 5-17), then click OK.

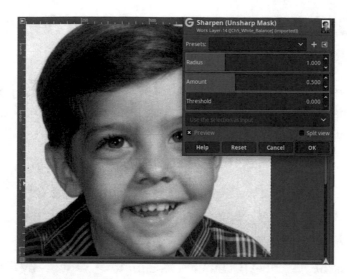

Figure 5-17. *Setting the Radius to 1.00 in the Unsharp Mask dialog*

Figure 5-18 shows the before and after comparison. When done, you can save as an .XCF file if you want to keep the file, or simply close it out.

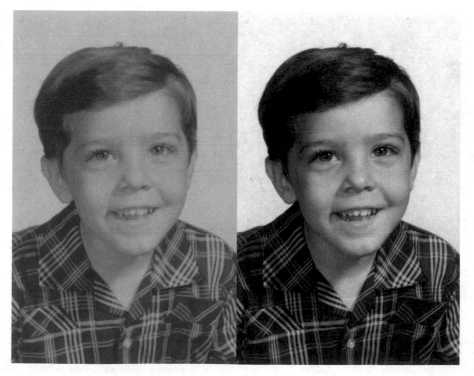

Figure 5-18. *The before and after comparison*

Tutorial 10: Turning a Color Image to Sepia Using Desaturate

If you want to recreate the old-fashioned look of sepia-toned photographs, it's easy to do using Glimpse. This method can be used on both color and black-and-white photographs in the RGB color mode.

1. Open the practice image *Ch5_Color_to_Sepia* in Glimpse.

2. Create a duplicate of the background layer (Right-Click ➤ Duplicate Layer) and rename it (*Work Layer*, or something similar).

3. Open the Sepia dialog (Colors ➤ Desaturate ➤ Sepia)—by ticking the *Split view* option, a side-by-side view comparing the effect applied shown against the original is displayed.

4. For the full sepia effect, leave the Effect Strength at the default setting of 1.00 (Figure 5-19), then click the OK button.

Figure 5-19. *Leaving at the default setting creates a full sepia effect*

5.   Now we'll sharpen the image just a bit. Open the Unsharp Mask
     dialog (Filters ➤ Enhance ➤ Sharpen (Unsharp Mask)).

6.   Set the Radius to 1.00, leaving Amount and Threshold at their
     default settings (Figure 5-20), then click OK.

Figure 5-20.   *Setting the Radius in the Unsharp Mask dialog*

Figure 5-21 shows the before and after comparison. When done, you can save as an
.XCF file if you want to keep the file, or simply close it out.

Figure 5-21.   *The before and after comparison*

The strength of the sepia effect can be varied. As Figure 5-22 shows, some color can show through if desired.

Figure 5-22. *The strength of the sepia effect can be varied*

Note   A sepia effect can also be achieved by desaturating the image (removing the color) and using the Colorize dialog (Colors ➤ Colorize). By using the Hue, Saturation, and Lightness sliders, it's possible to further customize the results.

Tutorial 11: Turning a Color Image to Black and White Using Mono Mixer

Glimpse makes it easy to convert a color image to black and white (grayscale, to be technically correct). Black and white gives an image a different "feel" than color. While you can just remove all of the color by turning the saturation level to zero, this doesn't always produce the best results without additional editing. The *Mono Mixer* dialog offers a great deal of control to fine-tune the results.

1. Open the practice image *Ch5_Color_to_Black_and_White* in Glimpse.

2. Create a duplicate of the background layer (Right-Click ➤ Duplicate Layer) and rename it (*Work Layer*, or something similar).

3. Open the Mono Mixer dialog (Colors ➤ Components ➤ Mono Mixer)—by ticking the *Split view* option, a side-by-side view comparing the effect applied shown against the original is displayed (Figure 5-23).

Figure 5-23. *The Mono Mixer dialog*

4. The default settings yield good results, but we'll make a couple of slight adjustments to create a little more contrast between the railroad ties and the grass growing between them.

5. As shown in Figure 5-24, adjust the *Red Channel Multiplier* to 0.75 and the Blue Channel Multiplier to 0.110—press OK when done.

Figure 5-24. *Adjusting the Red and Blue Channel Multipliers*

6.   Now we'll sharpen the image just a bit. Open the Unsharp Mask dialog (Filters ➤ Enhance ➤ Sharpen (Unsharp Mask)).

7.   Set the Radius to 1.00, leaving Amount and Threshold at their default settings, then click OK.

Figure 5-25 shows the before and after comparison. When done, you can save as an .XCF file if you want to keep the file, or simply close it out.

Figure 5-25. *The before and after comparison*

The Desaturate Dialog

Another method of converting color images into black and white is to use the Desaturate dialog (Colors ➤ Desaturate ➤ Desaturate). Figure 5-26 shows us the navigation sequence (yes, the word Desaturate is shown twice).

Figure 5-26. *Navigating to the Desaturate dialog*

The Desaturate dialog offers five options: *Luminance, Luma, Lightness (HSL), Average (HSI Intensity),* and *Value (HSV).* Figure 5-27 shows the differences in tonal values. These values are based upon mathematical calculations which are explained in detail in the GIMP user manual: `https://docs.gimp.org/2.10/en/gimp-filter-desaturate.html`.

Figure 5-27. *The different modes available in the Desaturate dialog*

Tutorial 12: Colorizing a Black-and-White Photo

Glimpse is a great program for colorizing black-and-white images. In the early days of photography before color film was widely used, black-and-white (or toned monochrome) images were colorized by using translucent oil-based dyes to provide an overlay of color. This tutorial is more or less the digital equivalent (but without the mess and more realistic results).

1. Open the practice image *Ch5_Colorize_Pendant* in Glimpse.

2. Create a duplicate of the background layer (Right-Click ➤ Duplicate Layer) and rename it (*Work Layer*, or something similar).

3. Normally, we save this for last, but for this tutorial, we'll sharpen the image just a bit at this point. Open the Unsharp Mask dialog (Filters ➤ Enhance ➤ Sharpen (Unsharp Mask)).

4. Set the Radius to 0.75, leaving Amount and Threshold at their default settings, then click OK.

5. Launch the New Layer dialog and create a new layer (Layer ➤ New Layer). This will be used to colorize the felt background under the pendant.

6. Name the layer Red Felt and change the blend mode to Multiply, then click OK. This blend mode will provide the felt a deep, rich scarlet/red color.

7. Launch the Color Selection dialog by clicking in the active foreground color swatch in the Toolbox.

8. Change the foreground color to 100% red by clicking and dragging to the upper-right corner as shown in Figure 5-28—press OK when done.

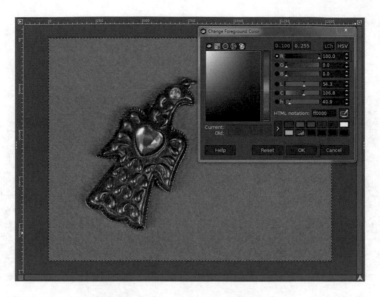

Figure 5-28. *Change the foreground color to 100% red*

9. Select the Paintbrush Tool (P) and choose a soft brush tip (Hardness 025). Change the diameter to about 15 pixels.

10. Paint an outline around the pendant.

11. Select the Fuzzy Select Tool (U). Change the Threshold to about 50, and click in an area just outside the outline (Figure 5-29). Make sure the selection is made on the layer named Red Felt.

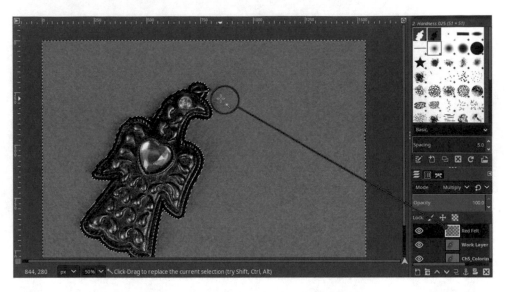

Figure 5-29. *Use the Fuzzy Select Tool to make a selection just outside of the outline around the pendant*

12. Before applying color, let's grow the selection a little to make sure the entire area is filled (Selection ➤ Grow). Enter a value of 5 pixels, then press OK when done (Figure 5-30).

Figure 5-30. *Use the Grow Selection dialog to make sure the entire area will be filled*

13. Fill the selected area with red (Edit ➤ Fill with FG Color), then
     deactivate the selection (Select ➤ None).

14. Duplicate the layer named Red Felt (Layer ➤ Duplicate), and
     change the blend mode to Overlay—reduce the opacity to 20%.

15. Launch the New Layer dialog and create a new layer (Layer ➤
     New Layer). This will be used to colorize the pendant.

16. Name the layer Bronze and change the blend mode to HSL Color.

17. Launch the Color Selection dialog by clicking in the active
     foreground color swatch in the Toolbox.

18. Change the foreground color to a bronze color by entering these
     values: R-23.1, G-17.6, and B-9.0 (Figure 5-31).

Figure 5-31. *Change the Foreground color to a bronze color using these
values*

19. Select the Paintbrush Tool (P) and choose a soft brush tip
     (Hardness 025). Apply the bronze color to the pendant, adjusting
     the brush size as needed.

20. Check your work by changing the blend mode to normal—the color will opaque and reveal any overlooked areas. Change the mode back to HLS Color when completely colorized.

21. Launch the New Layer dialog and create two new layers (Layer ➤ New Layer) for both the heart- and eye-shaped rhinestones; name one layer Heart and the other Eye.

22. Change the blend mode of the layer named Heart to HSL Color, and the layer named Eye to LCh Color.

23. Lower the opacity of each layer to 70% (this keeps the colors realistic looking and not overpowering).

24. Change the foreground color to a deep pink by entering these values: R-100, G-0, and B-41.6.

25. Select the Paintbrush Tool (P) and choose a soft brush tip (Hardness 025). Change the diameter to about 35 pixels, and apply the color in the heart-shaped rhinestone in the designated layer.

26. Change the foreground color to a light blue by entering these values: R-0, G-89.4, and B-100.

27. Select the Paintbrush Tool (P) and choose a soft brush tip (Hardness 025). Change the diameter to about 15–20 pixels, and apply the color in the eye-shaped rhinestone in the designated layer.

Figure 5-32 shows the before and after comparison. When done, you can save as an .XCF file if you want to keep the file, or simply close it out.

Figure 5-32. *The before and after comparison*

Chapter Conclusion

This chapter provided several tutorials on correcting color issues, as well as being a little artistic with color.

Here are the main topics that were covered:

- Correcting an unwanted color cast using Color Balance

- The Color Temperature dialog

- Correcting an image using Color Temperature

- Restoring faded color using Levels

- Restoring faded color using Auto White Balance

- Turning a color image to sepia using Desaturate

- Turning a color image to black and white using Mono Mixer

- Colorizing a black-and-white photo

In the next chapter, we'll look at modifying, retouching, and restoring damaged photos.

CHAPTER 6

Modifying, Retouching, and Restoring Photos

In this chapter, we'll now learn about modifying images (such as removing distracting objects or correcting a tilt in a building) to make them look their best.

The topics covered in this chapter are

Tutorial 13: Removing unwanted objects

Tutorial 14: Correcting perspective

Tutorial 15: Brightening teeth

Tutorial 16: Reducing wrinkles

Tutorial 17: Repairing scratches and damage

Chapter conclusion

Tutorial 13: Removing Unwanted Objects

Digitally removing unwanted objects is a common practice in image editing. It's best to remove distracting items that might appear in the background of the actual scene *before* the picture is taken—of course, this isn't always possible. In this lesson, we'll improve the image by removing the distracting items (the post and the metal dish), allowing the viewer to focus on the bird.

1. Open the practice image *Ch6_Remove_Objects* in Glimpse.

2. Create a duplicate of the background layer (Right-Click ➤ Duplicate Layer) and rename it (*Work Layer*, or something similar).

P. Whitt, *Practical Glimpse*, https://doi.org/10.1007/978-1-4842-6327-3_6

3. Select the Lasso Tool (L)—set the Feather Edges radius to 15, then select an area foliage just above the feeding dish (Figure 6-1).

Figure 6-1. *Use the Lasso Tool to select an area of foliage as shown*

4. We'll now copy this selection onto its own layer (first Edit ➤ Copy, then Edit ➤ Paste as ➤ New Layer). Rename the new layer Foliage.

5. Expand the layer boundary to match the image size by right-clicking the new layer's thumbnail preview and selecting Layer to Image Size from the menu (Figure 6-2).

Figure 6-2. *Increase the layer boundary to match the image size*

6. Deactivate the selection (Select ➤ Deselect).

7. Use the Move Tool (M) to position the layer down and slightly to the right to cover (most of) the dish and the post (Figure 6-3).

Figure 6-3. *Use the Move Tool to position the layer as shown*

8. Select the Clone Tool (C) and make sure Sample Merged is checked—pick the soft brush (2. Hardness 0.25) and adjust the diameter to about 150 pixels.

9. Use the Clone Tool to cover the exposed part of the metal dish (Figure 6-4).

Figure 6-4. *Use the Clone Tool to cover the exposed portion of the dish*

10. Lower the Foliage layer's opacity to about 70% (enough to see the layer below).

11. Switch to the Eraser Tool (Shift+E)—lower the brush diameter (about 40 pixels to work along the edge, larger the farther away from the edge you work) and remove the excess image area covering the bird (Figure 6-5). Increase the layer opacity to 100% when finished.

Figure 6-5. *Use the Eraser Tool to remove the excess image area covering the bird*

12. Click the Work Layer thumbnail to make the layer active.

13. Select the Lasso Tool (L)—set the Feather Edges radius to 15, then select an area foliage just to the right of the bird (Figure 6-6).

Figure 6-6. *Use the Lasso Tool to select an area just to the right of the bird*

14. We'll now copy this selection onto its own layer (first Edit ➤ Copy, then Edit ➤ Paste as ➤ New Layer). Rename the new layer Foliage 2.

15. Use the Move Tool (M) to position the layer above the bird (Figure 6-7).

Figure 6-7. *Use the Move Tool to position the layer as shown*

16. Lower the Foliage layer's opacity to about 70% (enough to see the layer below).

17. Switch to the Eraser Tool (Shift+E)—increase the brush diameter to about 150 pixels and remove the excess image area (Figure 6-8). Increase the layer opacity to 100% when finished.

Figure 6-8. *Use the Eraser Tool to remove the excess image area*

18.   Merge the two Foliage layers onto the Work Layer (Layer ➤ Merge Down).

19.   The last thing to do is to slightly sharpen the image. Open the Unsharp Mask dialog (Filters ➤ Enhance ➤ Sharpen (Unsharp Mask)).

20.   Set the Radius to 1.00, leaving Amount and Threshold at their default settings, then click OK.

Figure 6-9 shows the before and after comparison. When done, you can save as an .XCF file if you want to keep the file, or simply close it out.

Figure 6-9. *The before and after comparison*

Tutorial 14: Correcting Perspective

In this lesson, we'll use the *Unified Transform Tool* to correct the perspective of a small building. The church appears to be on a slant, but this will be a quick fix.

1. Open the practice image *Ch6_Slant_Fix* in Glimpse.

2. Create a duplicate of the background layer (Right-Click ➤ Duplicate Layer) and rename it (*Work Layer*, or something similar).

3. Select the Unified Transform Tool (Shift+T).

4. Click and drag the left upper corner straight up slightly, and the right upper corner down and to the right slightly—the roofline should look even (Figure 6-10). Click Transform when done.

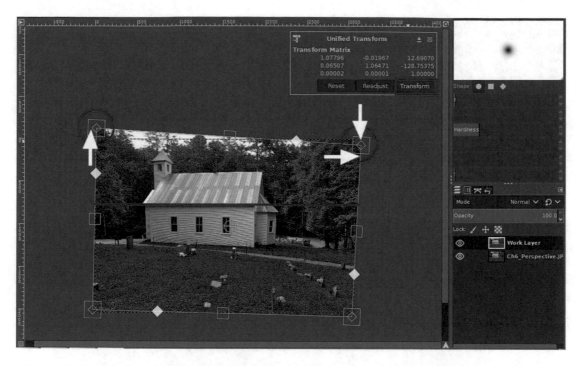

Figure 6-10. *Using the Unified Transform Tool to correct the image*

Tip   For even greater precision, a horizontal guide can be used to aid in leveling the roofline—click the horizontal ruler to drag it into place.

5. This action results in a couple of fairly obvious "seams" that will need to be corrected. They result because the Work Layer's edge is now at an angle, part of the background layer is revealed.

6. Create a new layer (Layer ➤ New Layer) and name it Clone— make sure the blend mode is set to Normal.

7. Select the Clone Tool (C) and make sure Sample Merged is checked—pick the soft brush (2. Hardness 0.25) and adjust the diameter to 23–25 pixels.

8. Use the Clone Tool to blend the grass over the seam in the lower-left corner (Figure 6-11).

Figure 6-11. *Removing a seam in the lower-left corner using the Clone Tool*

9.   Repeat this action in the upper-right corner (Figure 6-12).

Figure 6-12. *Removing a seam in the upper-right corner using the Clone Tool*

Note   In many instances, simply cropping the image will eliminate any seams and the need to use the Clone Tool—in this case cropping the image would have resulted in part of the steeple being cut off, so using the Clone Tool allowed me to preserve it.

Figure 6-13 shows the before and after comparison. When done, you can save as an .XCF file if you want to keep the file, or simply close it out.

Figure 6-13.   *The before and after comparison*

Tutorial 15: Brightening Teeth

Glimpse is a great program for retouching people to make them look their best. In this lesson, we'll use Glimpse to brighten teeth (they won't appear to be bleached, as in a glamour shot, just brightened enough to improve the image).

1.   Open the practice image *Ch6_Brighten_Teeth* in Glimpse.

2.   Create a duplicate of the background layer (Right-Click ➤ Duplicate Layer) and rename it (*Work Layer*, or something similar).

3.   Select the Lasso Tool (L)—set the Feather Edges radius to 3, then make a selection around the teeth (Figure 6-14).

Figure 6-14. *Use the Lasso Tool to make a selection around the teeth*

4. We'll now copy this selection onto its own layer (first Edit ➤ Copy, then Edit ➤ Paste as ➤ New Layer). Rename the new layer Brighter Teeth.

5. Open the Levels Dialog (Colors ➤ Levels), and move the white slider toward the left until the numeric value is 200 (Figure 6-15). Click OK when finished.

Figure 6-15. *Use the Levels Dialog to lighten the teeth a little*

6. We'll now reduce the color saturation of the teeth a bit. Open the
    Hue-Saturation dialog (Colors ➤ Hue-Saturation), and move the
    Saturation slider toward the left until the numeric value is −30
    (Figure 6-16).

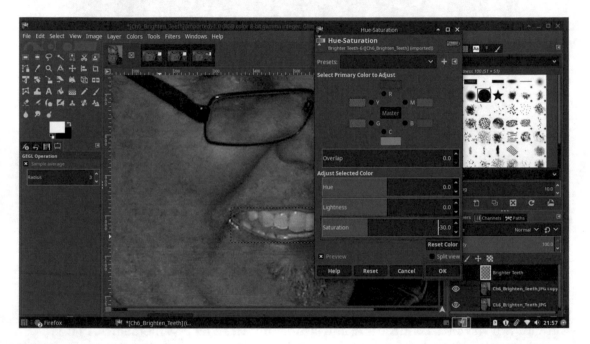

Figure 6-16. *Use the Hue-Saturation dialog to reduce the color saturation of the*
teeth a bit

7. Select the Eraser Tool (Shift+E)—using a small, soft brush, remove
    the excess pixels around the teeth.

8. Lower the opacity of the layer named *Brighter Teeth* to about 75%.

    Figure 6-17 shows the before and after comparison. When done,
    you can save as an .XCF file if you want to keep the file, or simply
    close it out.

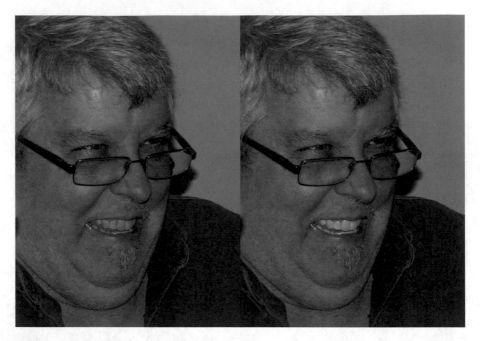

Figure 6-17. *The before and after comparison*

Tutorial 16: Reducing Wrinkles

Another way in which Glimpse is useful is to reduce wrinkles and blemishes. In this lesson, we'll use it to reduce the harshness in a few of the wrinkles of the woman in the photo. The retouching will be subtle.

1. Open the practice image *Ch6_Reduce_Wrinkles* in Glimpse.

2. Create a duplicate of the background layer (Right-Click ➤ Duplicate Layer) and rename it (*Work Layer,* or something similar).

3. Create a new layer (Layer ➤ New Layer) and name it Heal (or Wrinkles)—make sure the blend mode is set to Normal.

4. Lower the layer opacity to 65%.

5. Select the Healing Tool (H) and make sure Sample Merged is checked—pick the soft brush (2. Hardness 0.25) and adjust the diameter to 10–12 pixels.

6. Lower the brush opacity to 30%.

7. Click a source point, and work along the deepest wrinkles under
    the eyes (Figure 6-18). This doesn't completely eliminate them; it
    just reduces the harshness.

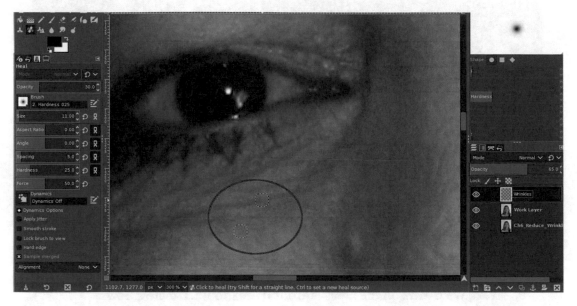

Figure 6-18. *Using the Healing Tool to reduce the harshness of the wrinkles*

8. After you've worked on the wrinkles under the eyes, use the
    Healing Tool on the birthmark next to the nose—again, this only
    diminishes it some (Figure 6-19).

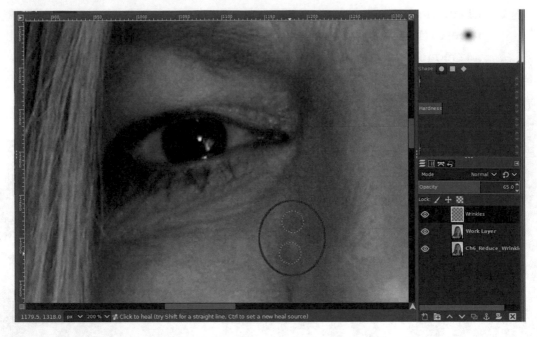

Figure 6-19. *Using the Healing Tool to diminish the birthmark*

9. Next, we'll work on the creases around the mouth. Create a new
    layer (Layer ➤ New Layer) and name it Creases—make sure the
    blend mode is set to Normal.

10. Change the brush size to around 22 pixels and the brush opacity
    to 50%.

11. Use the Healing Tool to reduce the harshness of the creases
    (Figure 6-20).

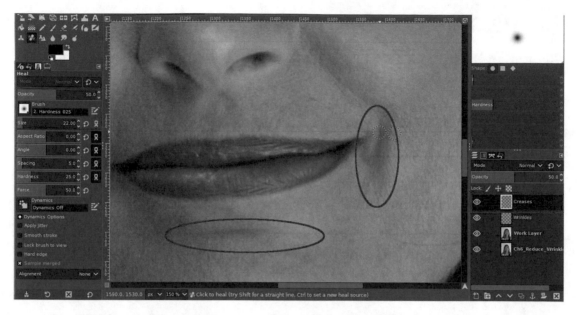

Figure 6-20. *Using the Healing Tool to diminish the creases*

Figure 6-21 shows the before and after comparison. When done, you can save as an .XCF file if you want to keep the file, or simply close it out.

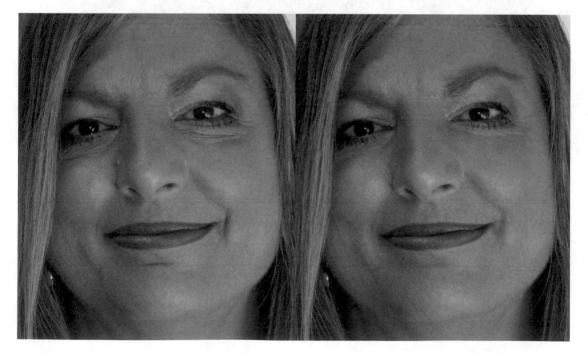

Figure 6-21. *The before and after comparison*

Tutorial 17: Repairing Scratches and Damage

Glimpse is a fantastic program for digitally restoring old photos that are damaged—it can be used to repair scratches, tears, spots, stains; just about any kind of damage except for extreme cases (when there's just too little to work with). In this lesson, we'll repair an old photograph from 1998 that sustained some damage over the years.

1. Open the practice image *Ch6_Damaged_Photo* in Glimpse.

2. Create a duplicate of the background layer (Right-Click ➤ Duplicate Layer) and rename it (*Work Layer*, or something similar).

3. The first thing to do is to patch the torn area on the left side. Select the Rectangle Select Tool (R)—set the Feather Edges radius to 10, then make a selection in the upper-left corner (Figure 6-22).

Figure 6-22. *Use the Rectangle Select Tool to select the area shown*

4. We'll now copy this selection onto its own layer (first Edit ➤ Copy, then Edit ➤ Paste as ➤ New Layer). Rename the new layer Repair Layer.

5. Use the Move Tool (M) to position the layer over the missing area
    (Figure 6-23).

Figure 6-23. *Use the Move Tool to position the layer over the missing area*

6. Lower the Repair Layer's opacity to about 80% (enough to see the
    layer below).

7. Expand the layer boundary to match the image size by right-
    clicking the new layer's thumbnail preview and selecting Layer to
    Image Size from the menu (Figure 6-2).

8. Select the Eraser Tool (Shift+E)—using the 2. Hardness 0.25 brush
    about 50 pixels in diameter, remove the excess pixels around the
    Repair Layer as shown in Figure 6-24, and restore layer opacity to
    100% when finished.

Figure 6-24. *Use the Eraser Tool to remove excess pixels from around the patched area*

9. Select the Clone Tool (C) and make sure Sample Merged is checked—pick the soft brush (2. Hardness 0.25) and adjust the diameter to about 35 pixels.

10. Use the Clone Tool to blend in the patched area with the surrounding pixels—be mindful of repeating patterns or areas that look obviously duplicated (Figure 6-25).

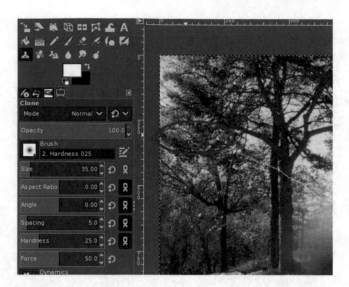

Figure 6-25. *Use the Clone Tool to blend pixels in from the surrounding area*

11. Use the Healing Tool (H) to work along the smaller scratch
    (Figure 6-26)—you may encounter areas in which the Healing
    Tool doesn't work well and will need to alternate between it and
    the Clone Tool.

Figure 6-26. *Use the Healing Tool to work along the smaller scratch, alternating with the Clone Tool as needed*

12.   Use the Clone Tool to work in the larger areas, increasing brush
      size as needed (Figure 6-27).

Figure 6-27. *Increase the Clone Tool's brush size as needed for working in larger areas*

13.   Use the Clone Tool to remove the time/date stamp in the lower-right corner (Figure 6-28).

Figure 6-28. *Use the Clone Tool to remove the time/date stamp*

14. Once the healing and cloning work is completed, merge the Repair Layer down onto the Work Layer (Layer ➤ Merge Down).

15. We'll now work on the areas with dust specks. Select the Lasso Tool (L)—set the Feather Edges radius to 5, then make a selection around the areas with the heaviest dust specks, such as the tree trunks and the open grassy area.

16. Launch the Despeckle Dialog (Filters ➤ Enhance ➤ Despeckle)— leave at the default settings and click OK (Figure 6-29).

Figure 6-29. *Use the Despeckle Dialog to remove the heaviest dust*

Figure 6-30 shows the before and after comparison. When done, you can save as an .XCF file if you want to keep the file, or simply close it out.

Figure 6-30. *The before and after comparison*

Chapter Conclusion

This chapter provided several tutorials on topics pertaining to modifying, retouching, and restoration.

Here are the main topics that were covered:

- Removing unwanted objects

- Correcting perspective

- Brightening teeth

- Reducing wrinkles

- Repairing scratches and damage

In the next chapter, we'll look at compositing images.

CHAPTER 7

Compositing Images

Compositing images essentially means borrowing various elements from other images to end up with a composite image. The two lessons that follow are an introduction to basic compositing (inserting the subject of one image into another).

The lessons covered in this chapter are

Tutorial 18: Adding a person to an image

Tutorial 19: Replacing backgrounds

Chapter conclusion

Note You'll notice that these two lessons are very similar, but they're approached differently in each case. Glimpse (in all of its complexity) allows the user different ways to achieve sImilar results—the more familiar the user becomes with different methods of achieving editing tasks, the more proficiency is gained.

Tutorial 18: Adding a Person to an Image

In this lesson, we'll take the image of a child and place it into another.

1. Open the practice images *Ch7_Teddy_Bear and Ch7_Child* in Glimpse.

2. If it isn't already, make *Ch7_Child* the active image (click the thumbnail in the Image Menu as shown in Figure 7-1).

© Phillip Whitt 2020
P. Whitt, *Practical Glimpse*, https://doi.org/10.1007/978-1-4842-6327-3_7

Figure 7-1. *Click the thumbnail preview to make the image active*

3. Open the Foreground Select Tool (click the tool icon as shown in
    Figure 7-2).

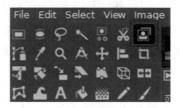

Figure 7-2. *Open the Foreground Select Tool by clicking the tool icon shown*

4. After the tool is launched (it looks like a lasso), draw around the
    child—it's a good idea to get as close as you can, but the selection
    does not have to be precise (Figure 7-3). After you've drawn
    around the child, press enter.

Figure 7-3. *Draw around the child as shown*

5. You'll now see a blue overlay around the selected area, with a lighter blue overlay over the selected area.

6. With the Draw foreground option selected, apply strokes in the image to select the child as shown in Figure 7-4—when the mouse button is released, the light blue overlay is removed.

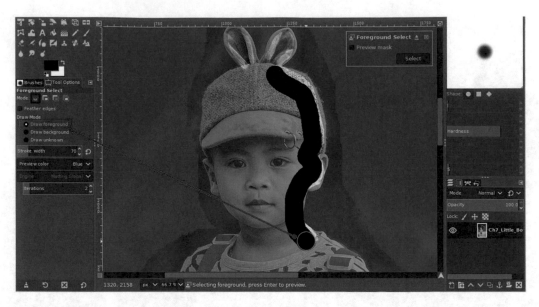

Figure 7-4. *Paint inside the child as shown*

Note   The Foreground Select Tool essentially calculates and differentiates between foreground and background pixels, so great precision isn't needed when painting in the foreground subject, but the more precise and thorough you can be, the better the selection will be.

---

7. Next, click the Draw background option, and paint around the subject as shown in Figure 7-5 (this applies the blue overlay a little closer to the subject)—when complete, click the Preview mask option.

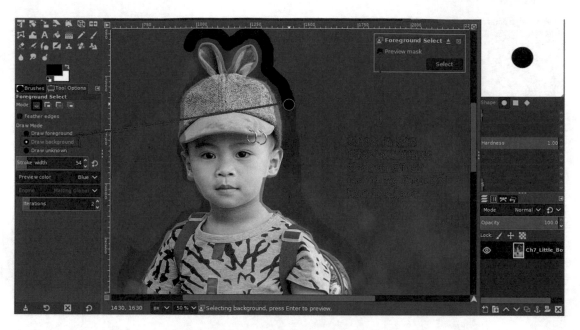

Figure 7-5. *Paint area around the child as shown, then tick the Preview mask option*

8. You will now see some stray "unknown" pixels that need to be cleaned up before a complete selection is made—tick the Draw foreground option to remove them from the subject, then tick the Draw background option to remove them from the background (Figure 7-6).

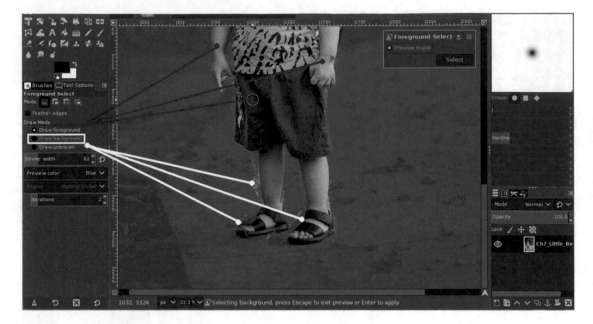

Figure 7-6. *Stray pixels that will need to be removed*

9.   Press the Select button—the subject will be selected
     (characterized by the boundary of "marching ants").

10. Toggle the Quick Mask (Select ➤ Toggle Quick Mask)—a red
     overlay is now applied, which reveals stray pixels that may have
     been overlooked (Figure 7-7). Paint (using white as the active
     foreground color) to remove any stray areas.

Figure 7-7. *Use the Quick Mask to reveal any overlooked areas*

11. Untick the Toggle Quick Mask option to switch to the "marching ants" selection.

12. Copy the selected area (Edit ➤ Copy).

13. Make the image *Ch7_Teddy_Bear* active by clicking the thumbnail preview in the Image Menu.

14. Paste as a new layer (Edit ➤ Paste As ➤ New Layer)—rename the layer Child.

15. Click the Scale Tool icon (or press Shift+S)—while holding the Shift key, click and drag the upper-left corner upward slightly to make the image slightly larger (about 1265 × 3617 pixels) as shown in Figure 7-8, then press the Scale button.

Figure 7-8. *Use the Scale tool to enlarge the subject slightly*

16. Use the Move Tool (M) to move the child up slightly as shown in
     Figure 7-9, then deselect.

Figure 7-9. *Move the subject into position as shown*

17. If you'll notice, the color temperature of the background image with the teddy bear is quite a bit warmer than the image the child was taken from, so we'll adjust the color temperature to get a better match between both elements.

Note Color Temperature (which is measured in Kelvin degrees) essentially means that lowering the temperature "cools" the tone, making cooler colors (such as bluish hues that might result from an incandescent light source) more prominent—increasing the color temperature "warms" the tone, making warmer colors (such as reddish hues resulting from early evening sunlight) more prominent.

---

18. Open the Color Temperature dialog (Colors ➤ Color Temperature)—making sure that the bottom layer is active, adjust the Intended temperature setting to 5000, which will make the warmer colors (reds, oranges) a little less prominent. Click OK when done (Figure 7-10).

Figure 7-10. *Adjusting the color temperature of the background image using the Color Temperature dialog makes it slightly cooler*

19. Now, we'll make a color temperature adjustment on the child. Open the Color Temperature dialog again (Colors ➤ Color Temperature)—making sure the top layer is active, set the Intended temperature slider to 9300, which will make the warmer colors (reds, oranges) more prominent. Click OK when done (Figure 7-11).

Figure 7-11. *Adjusting the color temperature of the layer containing the image of the child using the Color Temperature dialog makes it warmer*

20. Finally, select the Clone Tool (C), and remove the leaf (and the slight shadow cast by the leaf)—make sure the layer named Child is active (Figure 7-12).

Figure 7-12. *Remove the leaf and the slight cast shadow using the Clone Tool*

21. Figure 7-13 shows the before (the two original images) and after comparison (the final composite). When done, you can save as an .XCF file if you want to keep the file, or simply close it out.

Figure 7-13. *The before and after comparison*

Tutorial 19: Replacing Backgrounds

This lesson is similar to the previous one, in that a subject will be placed on a different image, resulting in a new background. The main differences are the subject will be a tropical bird, and the method of isolating the subject will be approached in a different manner.

1. Open the practice image *Ch7_Tropical_Background* in Glimpse.

2. Next, open the practice image *Ch7_Background_Change* as a layer, which will be placed on top of the previously opened image (File ➤ Open as Layers).

3. Using the Move Tool (M), position the subject to the left as shown in Figure 7-14—this will help compose the image following the rule of thirds.

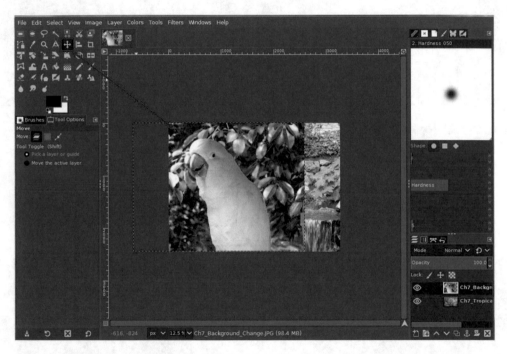

Figure 7-14. *Position the image as shown to follow the rule of thirds*

4. Add a layer mask to the layer initialized to white (full opacity), then press the Add button (Figure 7-15).

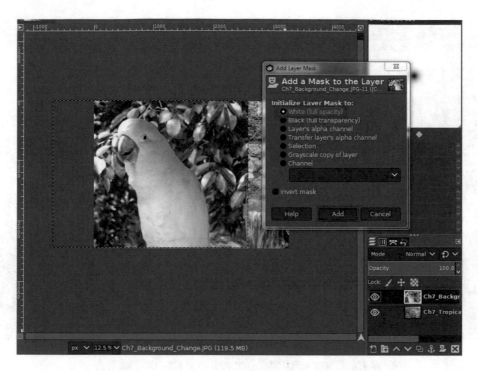

Figure 7-15. *Add a layer mask initialized to white*

5.   Using the Free Select Tool (F), draw around the foliage, getting as close to the bird as possible (Figure 7-16)—press enter after drawing the boundary to activate the selection.

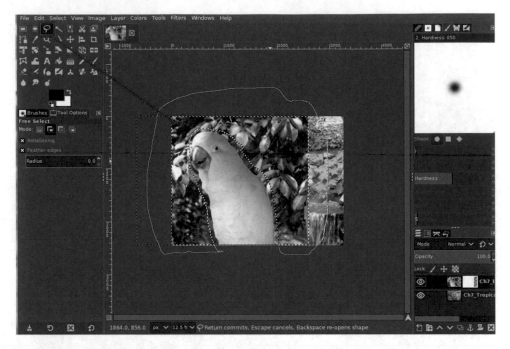

Figure 7-16. *Make a selection around the foliage as shown*

6. Click the layer mask preview thumbnail to make the layer mask active.

7. Fill the selection with black—this will reveal the visibility of most of the underlying background layer.

8. Select the Paintbrush Tool (P) and adjust the brush tip diameter to about 15 pixels (2. Hardness 0.50).

9. Paint along the edge of the bird to hide the stray background pixels, revealing the underlying background layer (Figure 7-17).

Figure 7-17. *Paint along using black to hide the stray pixels*

10. Zoom in as needed (Z) and check for any overlooked pixels—use the Paintbrush Tool to hide those until complete (Figure 7-18).

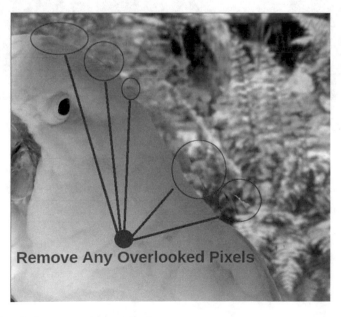

Figure 7-18. *Check for any stray pixels*

11. The last thing to do is to create a slight depth of field effect by blurring the background just a bit to put more emphasis on the bird.

12. Click the background layer to make it active (it will have the name Ch7_Tropical_Background).

13. Open the Gaussian Blur dialog (Filters ➤ Blur ➤ Gaussian Blur).

14. Set the x/y sizes to 5.00, then press OK (Figure 7-19).

Figure 7-19. *Creating a slight depth of field effect by blurring the background*

15. Figure 7-20 shows the before and after comparison. When done, you can save as an .XCF file if you want to keep the file, or simply close it out.

Figure 7-20. *The before and after comparison*

Chapter Conclusion

This chapter provided two lessons in creating basic composite images.
Here are the main topics that were covered:

- Adding a person to an image

- Replacing a background

In the next chapter, we'll explore some basic drawing using Glimpse.

PART III

Creating Digital Art

CHAPTER 8

Drawing Basics

Glimpse is a very capable program for tasks such as digital drawing and painting. With time and practice, you'll be able to create some impressive work.

In this chapter, we'll touch on drawing using the tools offered in Glimpse. This chapter is a primer to acquaint beginners with some of the tools available and a little firsthand experience.

We'll first take a closer look at the Pencil and Paintbrush tools and the various brush tips available.

The topics covered in this chapter are

- The Pencil and Paintbrush tools

- The MyPaint brush engine

- Tutorial 20: Drawing a simple flower

- Tutorial 21: Drawing a simple butterfly using symmetry painting

- Tutorial 22: Drawing a pattern using symmetry painting

- Chapter conclusion

The Pencil and Paintbrush Tools

The Pencil and Paintbrush tools in Glimpse were covered briefly in Chapter 3, but we'll have another quick recap before proceeding to the upcoming tutorials.

© Phillip Whitt 2020
P. Whitt, *Practical Glimpse*, https://doi.org/10.1007/978-1-4842-6327-3_8

Brush Tips

There are a variety of brush tip styles to simulate various media, such as acrylic, chalk, and so on. Figure 8-1 shows the Glimpse brush palette.

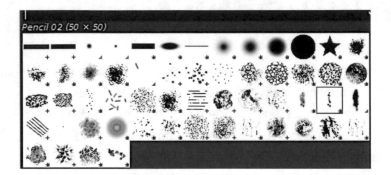

Figure 8-1. *The Glimpse brush palette*

The brush tips are available for all of the painting tools, but the behavior varies depending on the tool being used. Figure 8-2 shows the differences between the Pencil, Paintbrush, and Airbrush Tools simulating acrylic and chalk.

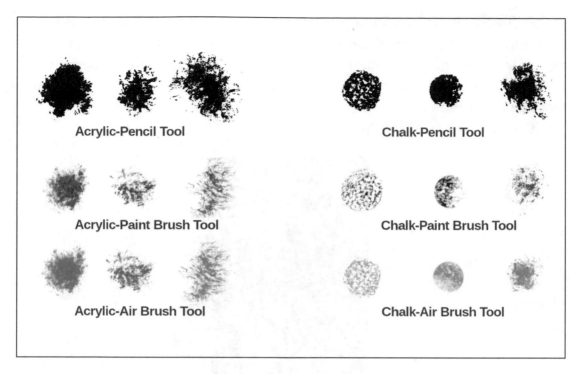

Figure 8-2. *A comparison of the results obtained from the Pencil, Paintbrush, and Airbrush Tools*

As was mentioned in Chapter 3, to use a drawing/painting tool freehand style, click and drag—to draw a straight line, hold the Shift key (Figure 8-3).

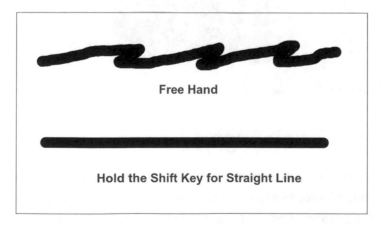

Figure 8-3. *A freehand stroke and a straight-line stroke*

The Tool Options allows you to adjust the brush parameters, such as size aspect ratio, angle, spacing, hardness, and force. The Brush Dynamics allows you to apply aspects to the brush stroke (such as jitter or smooth stroke). For most drawing purposes, I recommend using the smooth stroke—it's especially useful when using a mouse or a touch pad when drawing.

Figure 8-4 shows the Tool Options Panel.

Figure 8-4. *The Tool Options Panel*

The MyPaint Brush Engine

MyPaint is an open source painting program, but the brush engine is now included in both the GNU Image Manipulation Program (on which Glimpse is based) and Glimpse.

As good as the standard tools in Glimpse are, the MyPaint tools offer added flexibility, which will appear to those with drawing and painting experience. The MyPaint tools can be accessed in the toolbox as shown in Figure 8-5 or from the Tools Menu (Tools ➤ Paint Tools ➤ MyPaint Brush).

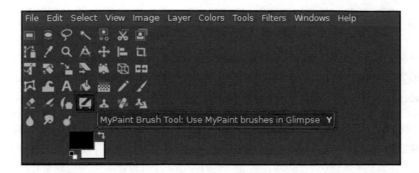

Figure 8-5. *The MyPaint tools can be accessed as shown or from the Tools Menu*

MyPaint tools mimic many of the real-world equivalents, such as acrylic, charcoal, chalk, watercolors, and more (Figure 8-6).

Figure 8-6. *The MyPaint tools menu*

Tutorial 20: Drawing a Simple Flower

This tutorial is probably the simplest one in this book. We'll be drawing a simple flower using digital pencil and chalk. It certainly won't be a masterpiece—it's primarily for new Glimpse users to become acquainted with the tools.

1. Create a new image (File ➤ New ➤ Create a New Image)—set the dimensions to 6" × 6" at 300 ppi.

2. Create a new layer (Layer ➤ New Layer), and in the New Layer dialog, rename it Flower Petals, then press OK.

3. Select the Pencil Tool (N)—choose the Pencil 03 brush, and change the size to 32 pixels.

4. Draw an outline similar to that shown in Figure 8-7.

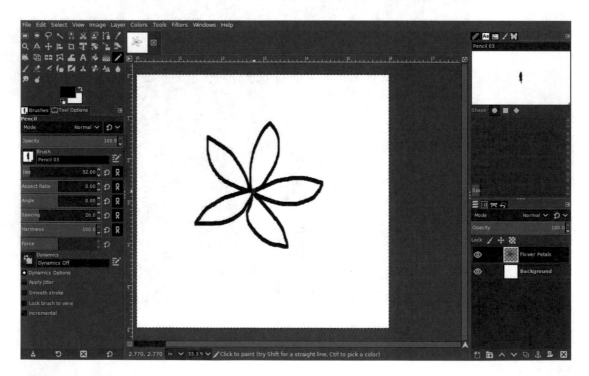

Figure 8-7. *Draw an outline similar to the one shown*

5. Lower the brush tip size to 15 pixels, and draw a line dividing the flower petals similar to that shown in Figure 8-8.

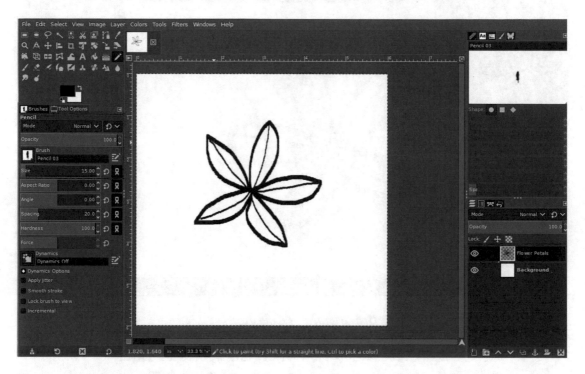

Figure 8-8. *Draw lines dividing the flower petals similar to that shown*

6. Create a new layer (Layer ➤ New Layer), and in the New Layer dialog, change the mode to LCh Color—rename the layer Flower Petal Color, then press OK.

7. Change the Pencil Tool brush tip to Chalk 02 and the brush size to 230 pixels.

8. Using yellow as the active color, fill in the flower petals (it's okay if it goes outside of the lines) as shown in Figure 8-9.

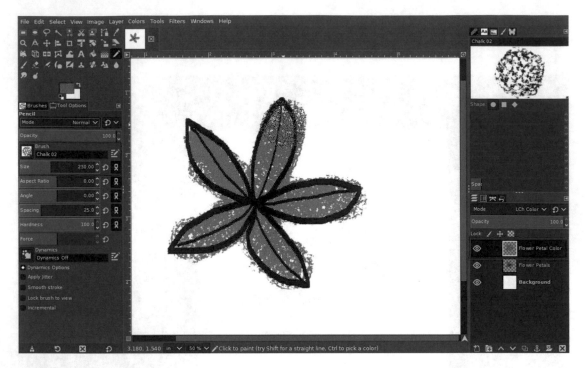

Figure 8-9. *Apply yellow to the drawing as shown*

9. Create a new layer (Layer ➤ New Layer), and in the New Layer dialog (leave the mode to LCh Color), rename the layer Flower Center, then press OK.

10. Change the foreground color to blue, then click a couple of times in the center of the flower as shown in Figure 8-10.

Figure 8-10. *Apply the blue in the center as shown*

Figure 8-11 shows the final result. When done, you can save as an .XCF file if you want to keep the file, or simply close it out.

Figure 8-11. *The final result*

Tutorial 21: Drawing a Simple Butterfly Using Symmetry Paint

This tutorial is a bit more involved than the previous one. However, this will introduce using Symmetry Paint to save time and effort.

In this tutorial, you'll work on an XCF file with a faint outline of a butterfly on the left side—when drawing over it using Symmetry Paint, it will automatically duplicate the effort on the right side, as will be seen shortly.

1. Open the .XCF file named Butterfly Drawing.

2. Create a new layer (Layer ➤ New Layer), and in the New Layer dialog (the mode should be set to normal), rename the layer Butterfly Outline, then press OK.

3. Launch the Symmetry Painting Dialog (Windows ➤ Dockable Dialogs ➤ Symmetry Painting).

4. Click the downward arrow on the top right area and choose Mirror—after this selection is made, enable the Vertical Symmetry option (a vertical dividing line is automatically placed in the center of the canvas).

5. Select the Pencil Tool (N)—choose the round brush (2. Hardness 100), and change the size to 5 pixels.

6. On the left size, draw over the faint gray outline—as you work, your efforts will be duplicated on the right side (Figure 8-12).

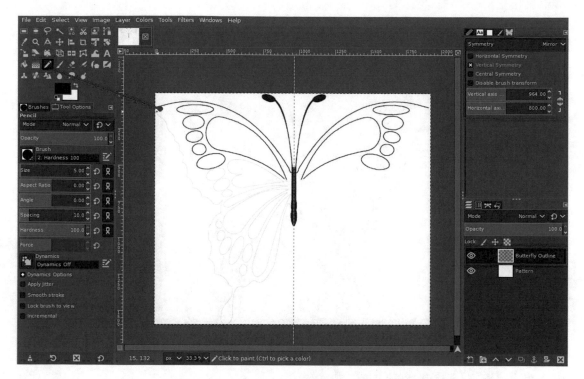

Figure 8-12. *When drawing on the left side over the gray pattern, the effort is duplicated on the right side*

7. When complete, the outline will look as the example shown in Figure 8-13.

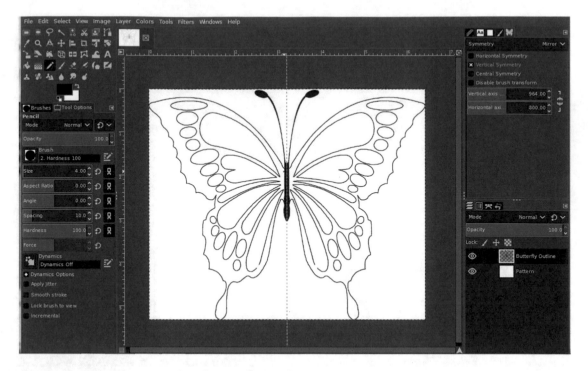

Figure 8-13. *The complete butterfly outline*

8. Now we'll fill in the areas surrounding the outline with some
    color—set the foreground color to yellow (R-100, G-100, B-100).

9. Select the Fuzzy Select Tool (U), then click just inside of the
    outline of the left wing—hold the Shift key and repeat on the right
    wing.

10. Fill the selected areas with the foreground color (Edit ➤ Fill with
    FG Color).

11. Deactivate the selection (Selection ➤ None)—the results should
    appear as shown in Figure 8-14.

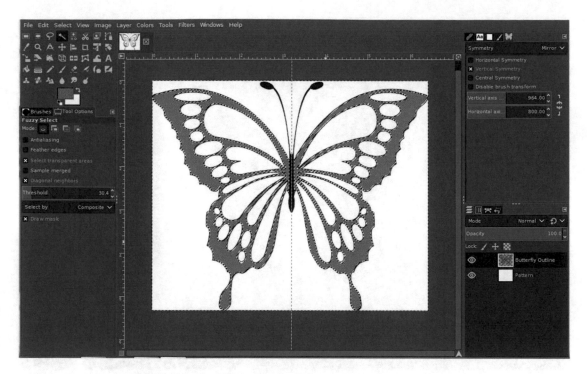

Figure 8-14. *Selected areas filled with yellow*

12. Change the foreground color to blue (R-0, G-0, B-100).

13. Select the Bucket Fill Tool (Shift+B), then click in the white areas
     within the butterfly until they are all filled (Figure 8-15).

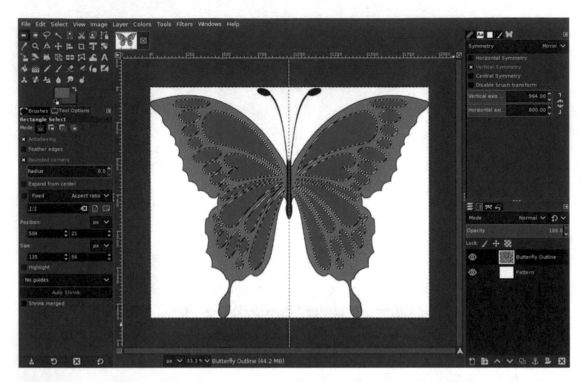

Figure 8-15. *Using the Bucket Fill Tool, fill the white areas within the butterfly with blue*

Figure 8-16 shows the final result. When done, you can save as an .XCF file if you want to keep the file, or simply close it out.

Figure 8-16. *The final result*

Tutorial 22: Drawing a Pattern Using Symmetry Paint

The previous segment showed how useful the Symmetry Paint Dialog can be. In the tutorial, we'll use it to draw a pattern (in this instance, don't worry too much about accuracy—achieving an approximate result will be fine).

1. Create a new image (File ➤ New ➤ Create a New Image)—set the dimensions to 6" × 6" at 300 ppi.

2. Create a new layer (Layer ➤ New Layer), and in the New Layer dialog, rename it Pattern, then press OK.

3. Launch the Symmetry Painting Dialog (Windows ➤ Dockable Dialogs ➤ Symmetry Painting).

4. Click the downward arrow on the top right area and choose Mandala—after this selection is made, a vertical and horizontal dividing line is automatically placed in the center of the canvas.

5. Select the Pencil Tool (N)—choose the hard, round brush tip (2. Hardness 100), and change the size to 10 pixels.

6. Using Figure 8-17 as a reference, start drawing upward from the bottom of the upper left quadrant in the direction indicated by the numbers and red lines (note the effort will be duplicated in the remaining areas).

Figure 8-17. *Draw a line as shown*

Figure 8-18 shows the complete pattern and how it resulted by drawing in the upper left quadrant.

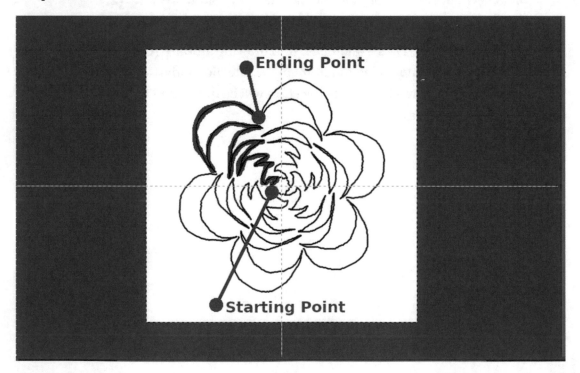

Figure 8-18. *The complete pattern*

Figure 8-19 shows the final result. When done, you can save as an .XCF file if you want to keep the file, or simply close it out.

Figure 8-19. *The final result*

Chapter Conclusion

In this chapter, there was a brief recap of the drawing, painting tools (specially, the Pencil and Paintbrush tools), and the tool options. We also created some work using the tools.

The topics covered in this chapter were

- The Pencil and Paintbrush tools

- The MyPaint brush engine

- Drawing a simple flower

- Drawing a simple butterfly using symmetry painting

- Drawing a pattern using symmetry painting

In the next chapter, we'll create some somewhat more advanced digital art using more of the features found in Glimpse.

CHAPTER 9

Creating Digital Artwork

In this chapter, we'll create some basic digital artwork using mostly selection tools, and filling the selections with various colors, gradients, and patterns. If you have little or no experience in creating graphics, this chapter will serve as an introduction.

Here are the topics covered:

> Raster vs. vector drawing
>
> Tutorial 23: Creating a sunny sky
>
> Tutorial 24: Creating a scenic sunset
>
> Tutorial 25: Drawing a retro TV set
>
> Chapter conclusion

Raster vs. Vector Drawing

Glimpse is primarily a photo editing program, but it does have the ability to create impressive *raster* graphics. One drawback to raster (or bitmap) graphics is that the work is composed of pixels and is not scalable without loss of sharpness—the more the image is enlarged, the softer it becomes (Figure 9-1). The edges may also become more jagged, which become apparent when the image is enlarged too much.

© Phillip Whitt 2020
P. Whitt, *Practical Glimpse*, https://doi.org/10.1007/978-1-4842-6327-3_9

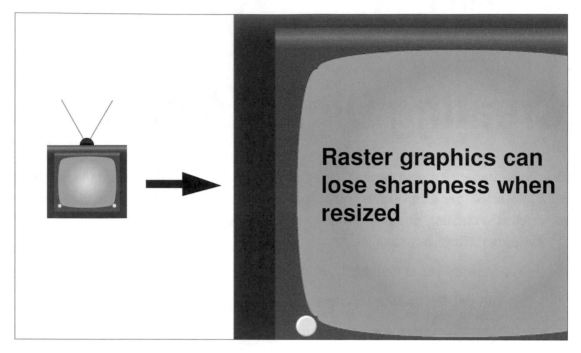

Figure 9-1. *Raster graphics can lose sharpness when enlarged*

Vector graphics (such as those created by programs like Inkscape, Adobe Illustrator, or Corel Draw) are composed of lines and paths which are scalable; they can be resized without loss of sharpness.

Vector programs are typically used by professional designers to create graphics for logos, line art, and other graphics that may need to be resized periodically. A vector drawing used as a logo in a business card can be upscaled to be used in a large poster—it will be just as crisp and sharp no matter how much it's enlarged (Figure 9-2).

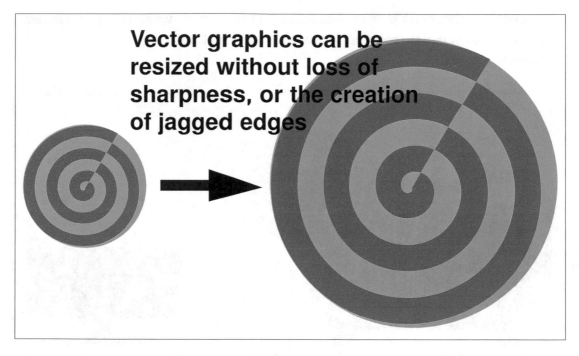

Vector graphics can be resized without loss of sharpness, or the creation of jagged edges

Figure 9-2. *Vector graphics are scalable, meaning they remain sharp no matter how much they are resized*

Of course, raster graphics still have practical use, and Glimpse is a great program for beginners to learn drawing basics. It also provides a means for nonprofessional graphic designers to create them on occasion—especially if resizing the graphic isn't an issue.

For example, even though I'm trained in both photo editing and graphic design, I work with digital photographs (which are raster images) far more often than digital drawings or illustrations. However, there are times I need to create graphics for a specific purpose.

Here's a case in point; in 2019, I authored a video tutorial for Apress Publishing titled *Digitizing and Enhancing Vintage Media with Adobe Photoshop Elements and Premier Elements*. As the long title suggests, it's about digitally preserving and improving vintage media, such as old photographs, slides, and home movies.

Because some of the equipment required for working with old home movies can still be acquired but is no longer manufactured, stock photos aren't readily available. I had a deadline to meet, so it was necessary for me to create graphics to illustrate several slides used in the production.

I used the program GNU Image Manipulation Program (on which Glimpse is based, and virtually identical) to create the graphics required for the presentation, one of which is shown in Figure 9-3.

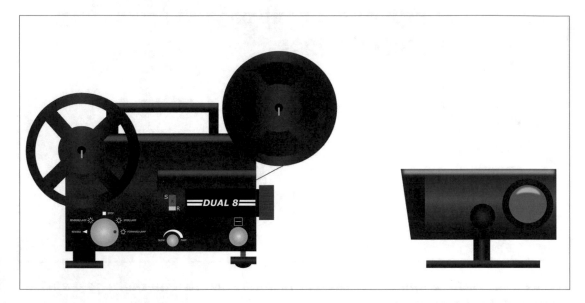

Figure 9-3. *This graphic for use in a presentation was created with GNU Image Manipulation Program (on which Glimpse is based)*

As mentioned earlier, Glimpse is mainly for editing digital photographs, but it can be used to produce nice raster graphics—ideal for beginners, or those who need to create non-scalable illustrations on occasion.

Tutorial 23: Creating a Sunny Sky

In this tutorial, we'll create a depiction of a sunny day.

1. First, let's change the background color to a blue for the sky. Click the active background color to launch the Change Background Color dialog—change red to 24.8%, green to 57.3%, and blue to 100%, then press OK (Figure 9-4).

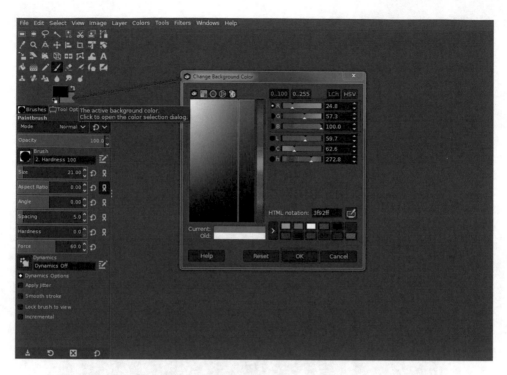

Figure 9-4. *Set the background color as shown*

2. You'll need to create a new blank image (File ➤ New)—when the Create a New Image dialog launches, set the dimensions to 10 inches by 8 inches. Set the x/y resolutions to 300 ppi, then press OK (Figure 9-5).

Figure 9-5. *Set the dimensions and x/y resolutions as shown*

3. After the new image is created, place a vertical guide at the 5"
    mark and a horizontal guide at the 4" mark—they should intersect
    in the exact center (Figure 9-6).

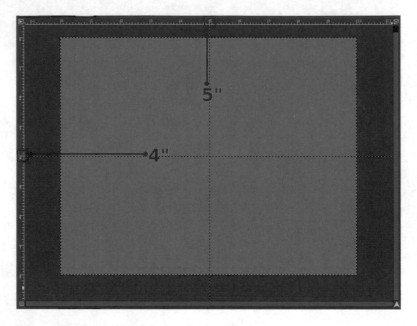

Figure 9-6. *Place guides in image as shown*

4. Create a new layer (Layer ➤ New Layer), and in the New Layer
    dialog, rename it Rays, then press OK.

5. Change the foreground color to yellow by clicking in the active
    foreground color to launch the Change Foreground Color dialog—
    change red to 100%, green to 100%, and blue to 0%, then press OK
    (Figure 9-7).

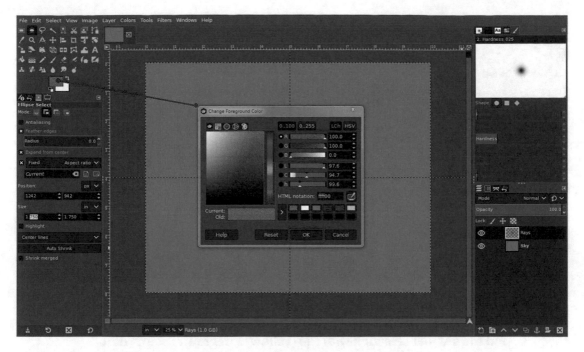

Figure 9-7. *Set the foreground color as shown*

6. Using the Ellipse Select Tool (E), we'll draw a circle in the center of
    the image on the layer named Rays.

7. With the Antialiasing box ticked, Expand from center, and Fixed
    (Aspect Ratio) boxes ticked, click and drag from the intersection
    point of the guides and make a circular selection about 2" in
    diameter (Figure 9-8).

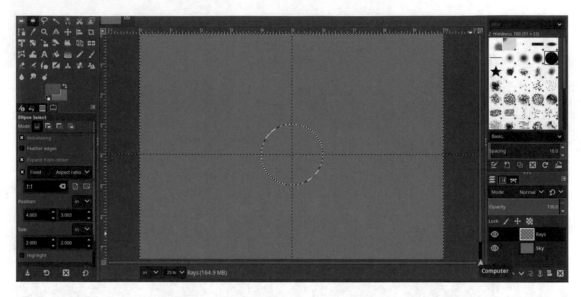

Figure 9-8. *Make a circular selection about 2" in diameter as shown*

8.   Fill the circular selection with the (yellow) foreground color (Edit ➤ Fill with FG Color).

9.   Deactivate the selection (Selection ➤ None).

10.   Open the Gaussian Blur dialog (Filters ➤ Blur ➤ Gaussian Blur).

11.   Set the x/y sizes to 100, then click OK (Figure 9-9).

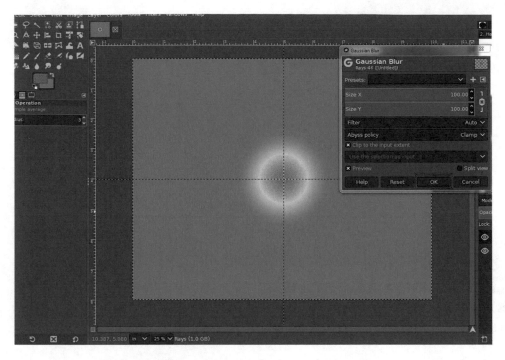

Figure 9-9. *Set the Gaussian Blur to 100 on the x/y sizes*

12.   Select the Pencil Tool (N)—choose the 2. Hardness 100 brush, and make the thickness 5 pixels.

13.   While holding the Shift key, draw a total of 8 lines around the blurred circle on the layer named Rays, intersecting in the center as shown in Figure 9-10—imagine cutting a pie into 16 pieces.

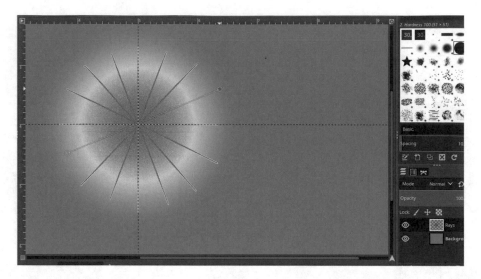

Figure 9-10. *While holding down the Shift key, use the Pencil Tool (N) to draw lines as shown*

14. Open the Gaussian Blur dialog (Filters ➤ Blur ➤ Gaussian Blur).

15. Set the x/y sizes to 25–27, then click OK—this will blur the lines to create the sun rays (Figure 9-11).

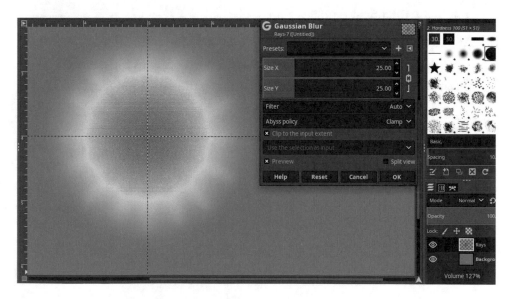

Figure 9-11. *Use the Gaussian Blur dialog to blur the lines, creating the sun rays*

16.   Create a new layer (Layer ➤ New Layer) and name it Inner Orb.

17.   Using the Ellipse Select Tool (E), we'll draw a circle in the center of the sun illustration on the new layer.

18.   With the Feather Edges radius set to 25, click and drag from the center and make a selection about 1" in diameter and fill it with white (Figure 9-12).

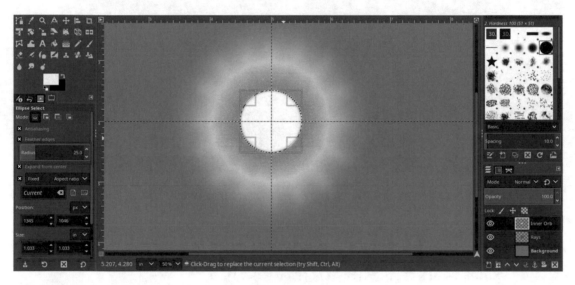

Figure 9-12. *Make a white circle as shown*

19.   Deactivate the selection (Select ➤ None).

20.   Open the Gaussian Blur dialog (Filters ➤ Blur ➤ Gaussian Blur).

21.   Set the x/y sizes to 50, then click OK.

22.   Merge the Inner Orb layer down onto the Rays layer (Right-Click ➤ Merge Down).

23.   Use the Move Tool (M) to move the newly merged layer to the center of the upper left quadrant.

24.   Merge the layer onto the background (Sky) layer (Right-Click + Merge Down).

25.   Select the Paintbrush Tool (P) and choose the Smoke tip— increase the brush size to about 2700 pixels (it can be close).

26.   Using white as the active color, click to dab clouds in the areas
       shown in Figure 9-13.

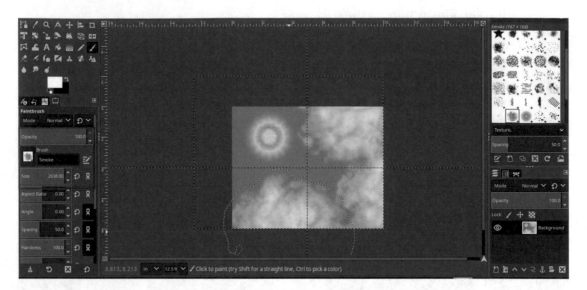

Figure 9-13. *Use the Smoke brush tip to paint in clouds*

27.   Finally, we'll add a lens flare for added effect—open the Lens Flare
       dialog (Filters ➤ Light and Shadow ➤ Lens Flare) and set the x/y
       positions at 0.75, then click OK (Figure 9-14).

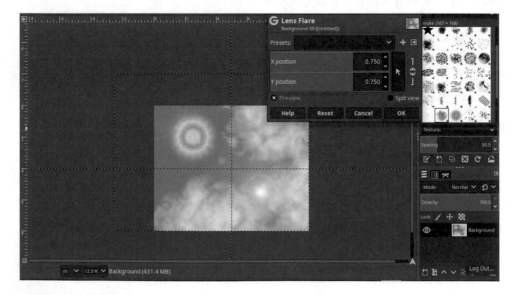

Figure 9-14. *Applying a Lens Flare filter for added effect*

Figure 9-15 shows the final result. When done, you can save as an .XCF file if you want to keep the file, or simply close it out.

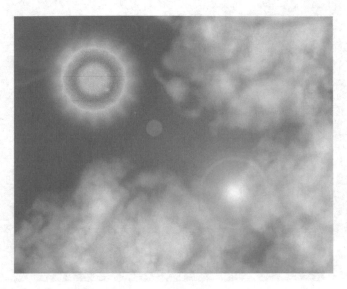

Figure 9-15. *The final result*

Tutorial 24: Creating a Scenic Sunset

In this tutorial, we'll create a depiction of a sunset over a mountain range.

1. Create a new image (File ➤ New ➤ Create a New Image)—set the dimensions to 10" × 8" at 300 ppi—rename the background layer Sunset Background.

2. Set the foreground color to an orange hue (R-100, G-50.2, B-0.00) and the background color to a yellow hue (R-89.4, G-89.4, B-0.00).

3. Using the Gradient Tool set to Linear, draw a transition from orange to yellow as shown in Figure 9-16.

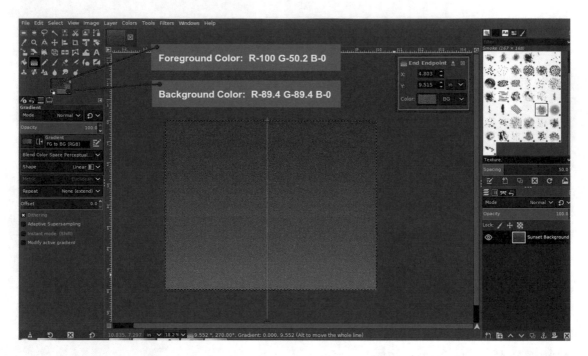

Figure 9-16. *Creating a transition from orange to yellow*

4. Create a new layer (Layer ➤ New Layer) and name it Sun.

5. Using the Ellipse Select Tool, make a circular selection about 5" in
    diameter placed in the lower portion as shown in Figure 9-17—
    make sure to use the following settings:

    • Feather Edges-Radius-25

    • Expand from center

    • Aspect ratio-fixed

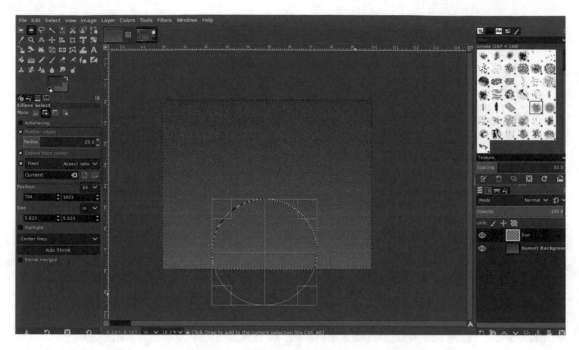

Figure 9-17. *Make a circular selection as shown*

6. Fill the selection with the orange foreground color (Edit ➤ Fill with FG Color), then deactivate the selection (Select ➤ None).

7. Change the foreground color to 50% gray (R-50, G-50, B-50) and the background color to 85% gray (R-15, G-15, B-15).

8. Create a new layer (Layer ➤ New Layer), and name it Mountains 1.

9. Using the Free Select Tool (F) with the Feather Edges radius set to 5, make a jagged selection to represent a mountain range similar to that shown in Figure 9-18.

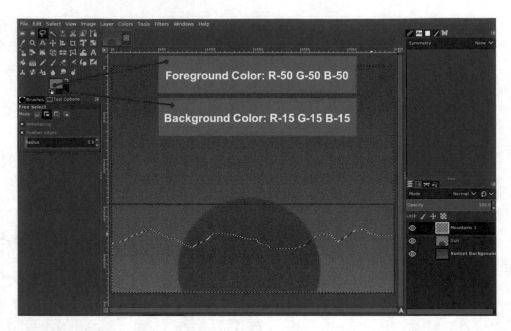

Figure 9-18. *Use the Free Select tool to make a selection to use for mountains*

10. Fill with the light gray foreground color (Edit ➤ Fill with FG Color), then deactivate the selection (Selection ➤ None).

11. We'll repeat steps 9 and 10, naming the new layer Mountains 2 and filling the selection with the dark gray background color (Figure 9-19).

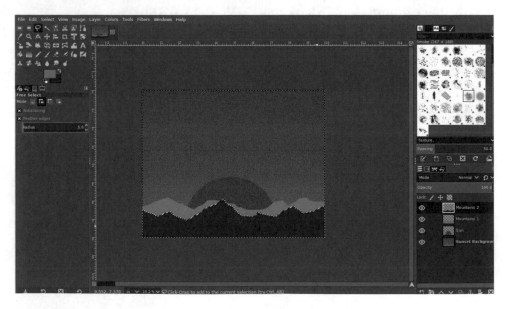

Figure 9-19. *Fill the second selection with the darker gray*

12. Deactivate the selection (Selection ➤ None).

13. Create a new layer and name it clouds.

14. Using the Paintbrush Tool (P) and dark gray as the foreground
     color, click once to paint a cloud with the Smoke brush tip set to
     4000 pixels in size (Figure 9-20).

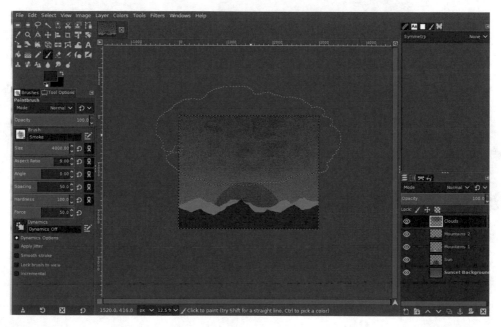

Figure 9-20. *Use the Smoke paintbrush tip for the cloud*

Figure 9-21 shows the final result. When done, you can save as an .XCF file if you
want to keep the file, or simply close it out.

Figure 9-21. *The final result*

Tutorial 25: Creating a Retro TV Set

In this tutorial, we'll create an illustration of a retro-style TV set. This lesson will be a little more in depth than the other two, so I created an .XCF file (with the necessary guides and layers in place) that should help save a bit of time.

1. Open the practice image *Ch_9_Dark_Retro_TV* in Glimpse.

2. Set the foreground color to a pink hue (R-100, G-55, B-55.2) and the background color to red (R-100, G-0, B-0).

3. Click the layer preview thumbnail named Cabinet to make it active.

4. Using the Rectangle Select Tool (with the Feather Edges option unticked), draw a selection around the outermost vertical and horizontal guides (Figure 9-22). Leave the selection active.

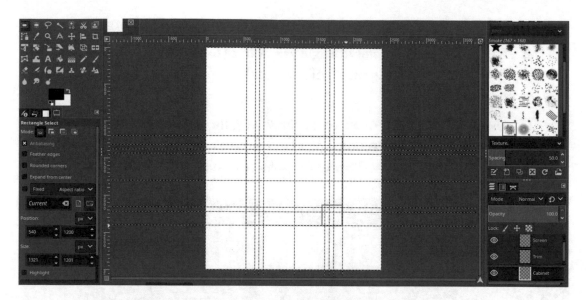

Figure 9-22. *Draw a rectangular selection along the outermost guides*

5. Select the Gradient Tool (G) using the FG to BG setting and the Bi-linear shape, make a gradient as shown in Figure 9-23—this will give the cabinet a slight reflection along the top.

6. Deactivate the selection (Selection ➤ None).

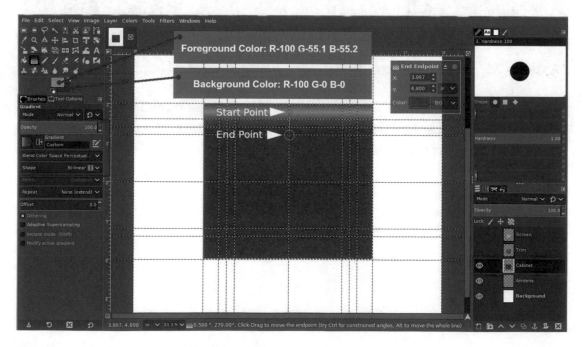

Figure 9-23. *Draw a gradient as shown*

7. Click the layer preview thumbnail named Trim to make it active.

8. Set the foreground color to a light yellow hue (R-99.3, G-88.7, B-40.7) and the background color to a darker yellowish-gold (R-86.8, G-88.7, B-5.2).

9. Using the Rectangle Select Tool (with the Feather Edges option unticked), draw a selection around the second outermost vertical and horizontal guides (Figure 9-24)—leave the selection active.

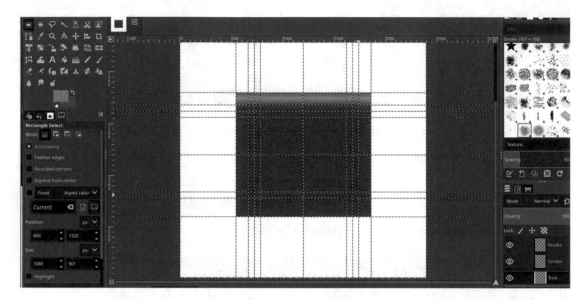

Figure 9-24. *Draw a rectangular selection along the second outermost guides*

10. Select the Gradient Tool (G) using the FG to BG setting and the Bi-linear shape, make a gradient as shown in Figure 9-25—this will give the trim a slight reflection along the top.

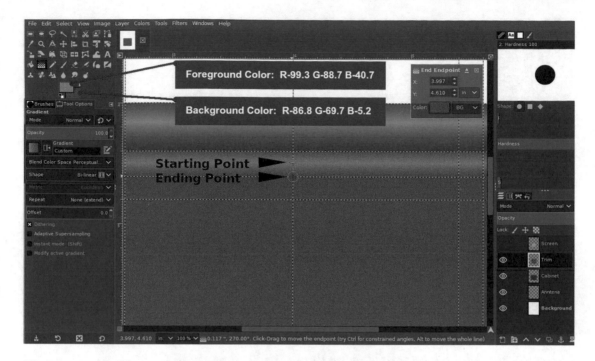

Figure 9-25. *Draw a gradient to create the trim as shown*

11. Click the layer preview thumbnail named Screen to make it active.

12. To draw the screen (or picture tube as they were called on older
     television sets), select the Paths Tool (B) and place nodes along
     the guides, and in the order shown in Figure 9-26—place the fifth
     node just under the first one, then click it and drag upward to
     complete the rectangular path.

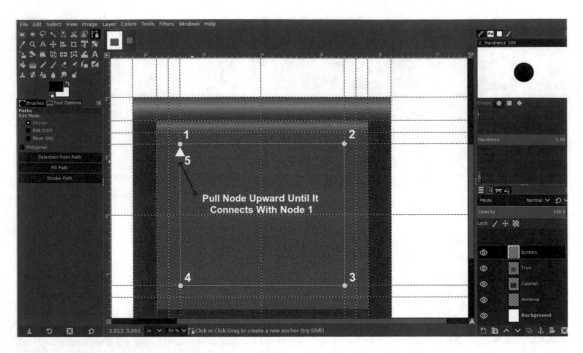

Figure 9-26. *Make a rectangle using the Paths Tool as shown*

13. Click each side (in the center) and curve outward as shown in Figure 9-27.

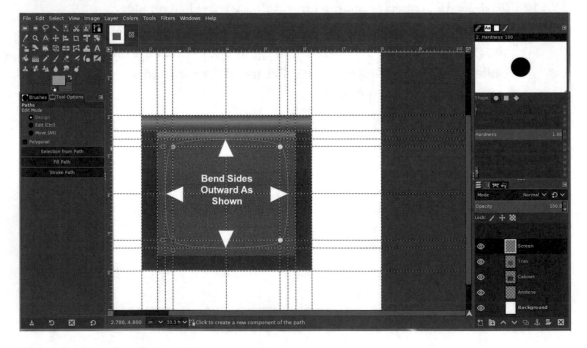

Figure 9-27. *Bend the sides outward as shown*

14. Turn the path into a selection (Select ➤ From Path).

15. Set the foreground color to a very light gray (R-92, G-92, B-92) and the background color to a darker gray (R-65, G-65, B-65).

16. To fill in the screen, select the Gradient Tool (G) using the FG to BG setting and the Radial shape, make a gradient (starting from the center) as shown in Figure 9-28.

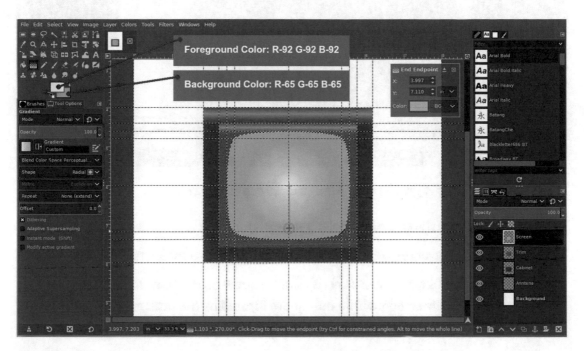

Figure 9-28. *Draw a gradient to fill in the screen as shown*

17. Open the Add Bevel dialog (Filters ➤ Decor ➤ Add Bevel).

18. Use the default Thickness setting of 5 and click OK. This gives the image a more 3-D appearance (Figure 9-29).

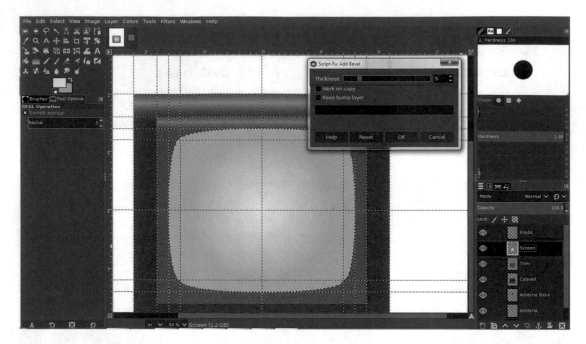

Figure 9-29. *Draw a gradient to fill in the screen as shown*

19. Deactivate the selection (Selection ➤ None).

20. Click the layer preview thumbnail named Knobs to make it active.

21. Using the Ellipse Select Tool (E), draw a circle on the bottom left
     corner of the screen within the square formed by the intersecting
     guides—be sure to use the following settings:

     - Antialiasing option ticked

     - Feather Edges option unticked

     - Expand from center

     - Aspect ratio-fixed

22. Hold the Shift key down and draw a circle in the lower right-
     hand area near the screen (look for the square formed by the
     intersecting lines).

23. Fill the selections using the same light gray that was used in the
     previous gradient.

24. Open the Add Bevel dialog (Filters ➤ Decor ➤ Add Bevel).

25. Use the default setting of 5 (Thickness) and click OK. This gives the knobs a more 3-D appearance (Figure 9-30).

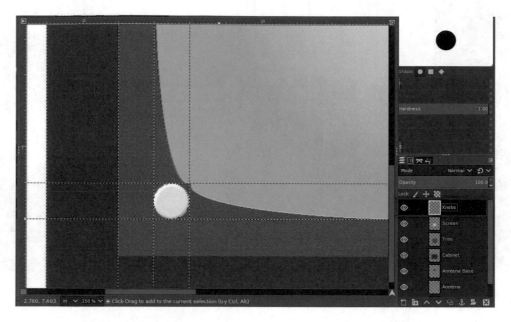

Figure 9-30. *Adding a bevel to the knobs gives a more 3-D appearance*

26. Open the Add Bevel dialog (Filters ➤ Decor ➤ Add Bevel).

27. Use the default Thickness setting of 5 and click OK. This will give the knobs a more 3-D appearance.

28. Click the layer preview thumbnail named Antenna Base to make it active.

29. Using the Ellipse Select Tool (E), draw about .80 inches in diameter with the top half extending from the top of the TV cabinet.

30. Change the foreground color to a dark gray, and use black for the background color.

31. Select the Gradient Tool (G) using the FG to BG setting and the Bi-linear shape, make a gradient as shown in Figure 9-31—this will give the base a slight reflection.

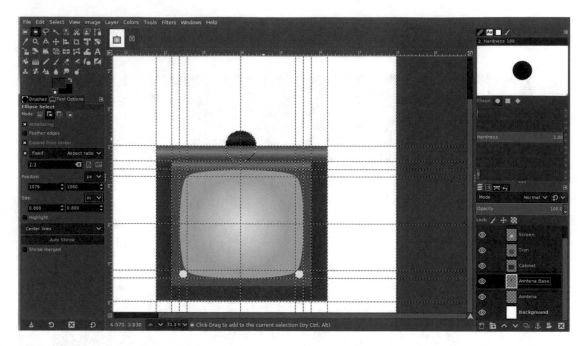

Figure 9-31. *Apply a gradient to the antenna base as shown*

32. Click the layer preview thumbnail named Antenna to make it active.

33. Using the Pencil Tool (N) with a hard brush tip 12 pixels in diameter, click and hold the Shift key and draw two straight lines for the antenna as shown in Figure 9-32.

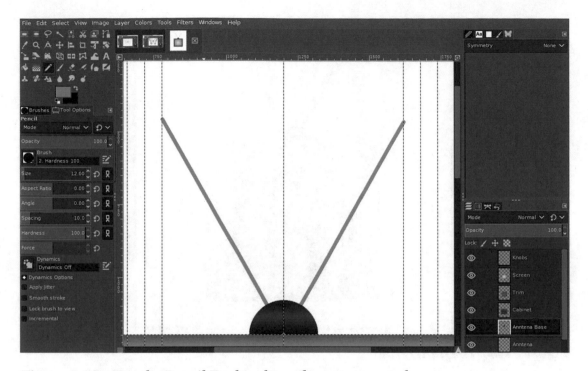

Figure 9-32. *Use the Pencil Tool to draw the antenna as shown*

Figure 9-33 shows the final result. When done, you can save as an .XCF file if you want to keep the file, or simply close it out.

Figure 9-33. *The final result*

Chapter Conclusion

This chapter provided three tutorials on creating digital artwork using Glimpse.

Here are the main topics that were covered:

- Raster vs. vector graphics

- Creating a sunny sky

- Creating a scenic sunset

- Drawing a retro TV set

In the next and final chapter, we'll look at using filters to turn photos into digital artwork with ease.

CHAPTER 10

Using Artistic Filters

Glimpse offers a wide assortment of filters for creating various effects. In this chapter, the focus will be on the artistic filters for turning photos into works of art.

The lessons covered in this chapter are

> Tutorial 26: Turn a photo into a digital oil painting
>
> Tutorial 27: Turn a photo into a digital watercolor
>
> Tutorial 28: Turn a photo into a digital pen and ink drawing
>
> Tutorial 29: Turn a photo into a Warhol-like painting
>
> Tutorial 30: Combine two images to create a digital mural

Note   You'll notice that the Artistic Filters menu has some of the same effects shown twice—one is the GEGL version, and the other Legacy version. GEGL (which stands for Generic Graphics Library) supports higher bit-depth images and displays on canvas previews.

Here are the topics that will be covered in this chapter:

1. Downloading and installing Glimpse

2. An overview of the workspace

3. Customizing the workspace

4. Menus, windows, and dialogs

Now, let's proceed to the first tutorial in this chapter. By the way, the artistic filters are fun—please do follow the instructions, but experiment with the filters when you're done and enjoy!

© Phillip Whitt 2020
P. Whitt, *Practical Glimpse*, https://doi.org/10.1007/978-1-4842-6327-3_10

Tutorial 26: Turn a Photo into a Digital Oil Painting

In this lesson, the *Oilify* and *Apply Canvas* filters will be used to turn a photo into a digital oil painting.

1. Open the practice image *Ch_10_Dogwood_Tree* in Glimpse.

2. Create a duplicate of the background layer (Right-Click ➤ Duplicate Layer) and rename it (*Work Layer*, or something similar).

3. Click the duplicate layer icon to make it active.

4. Launch the Oilify filter dialog (Filter ➤ Artistic ➤ Oilify).

5. Change the values in the dialog as follows:

    •   Mask Radius—12

    •   Exponent—8

    •   Number of intensities—90

These values can be seen in Figure 10-1.

Figure 10-1. *Use these values in the Oilify Dialog*

6. Click OK to apply the filter.

7. Now we'll apply a light canvas texture to the image to add more realism. Launch the Apply Canvas dialog (Filter ➤ Artistic ➤ Apply Canvas).

8. Use the default settings as shown in Figure 10-2. If for some reason the settings are different when you launch the dialog, set them as follows:

    •   Direction—Top-right

    •   Depth—4

Figure 10-2.   *Use these values in the Apply Canvas dialog*

9. Figure 10-3 shows the before and after comparison. When done, you can save as an .XCF file if you want to keep the file, or simply close it out.

Figure 10-3. *The before and after comparison*

Tutorial 27: Turn a Photo into a Digital Watercolor

In this lesson, the *Waterpixels* and *Clothify* filters will be used to turn a photo into a digital watercolor painting.

1. Open the practice image *Ch_10_Flowers* in Glimpse.

2. Create a duplicate of the background layer (Right-Click ➤ Duplicate Layer) and rename it (*Work Layer*, or something similar).

3. Click the duplicate layer icon to make it active.

4. Launch the Waterpixels filter dialog (Filter ➤ Artistic ➤ Waterpixels).

5. Use the default settings as shown in Figure 10-4. If for some reason the settings are different when you launch the dialog, set them as follows:

   • Superpixels size—32

   • Gradient smoothness—1.00

   • Spatial regularization—0

   • Superpixels color—Average

Figure 10-4. *Use these values in the Waterpixels dialog*

6. Now we'll apply a light cloth texture to the image to add more realism. Launch the Clothify dialog (Filter ➤ Artistic ➤ Clothify).

7. Use the settings as follows (shown in Figure 10-5):

   - Blur X—9

   - Blur Y—9

   - Azimuth—135.0

   - Elevation—45.0

   - Depth—1

Figure 10-5. *Use these values in the Clothify dialog*

8. Figure 10-6 shows the before and after comparison. When done, you can save as an .XCF file if you want to keep the file, or simply close it out.

Figure 10-6. *The before and after comparison*

Tutorial 28: Turn a Photo into a Digital Pen and Ink Drawing

In this lesson, *Posterize* and *Clothify* filters will be used to turn a photo into a digital pen and ink drawing.

1. Open the practice image *Ch_10_Yellow_Flower* in Glimpse.

2. Create a duplicate of the background layer (Right-Click ➤ Duplicate Layer) and rename it (*Work Layer*, or something similar).

3. Click the duplicate layer icon to make it active.

4. Launch the Posterize dialog (Colors ➤ Posterize). This will reduce the number of colors in the image, making it look more like a drawing than a photograph.

5. Set the Posterize levels to 5 (Figure 10-7), then click OK.

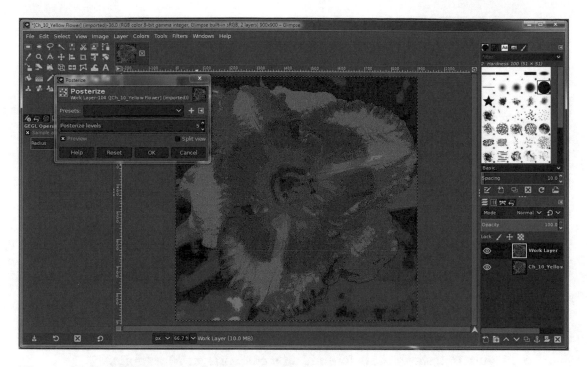

Figure 10-7. *The Posterize levels set to 5*

6. Launch the Cartoon filter (Filter ➤ Artistic ➤ Cartoon).

7. Use the settings as follows (shown in Figure 10-8):

   - Mask radius—7.0

   - Percent black—0.200

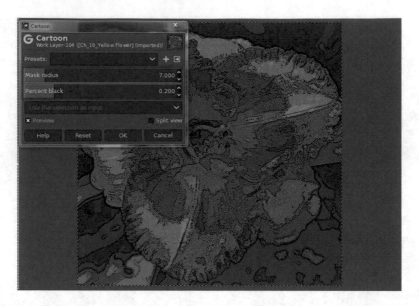

Figure 10-8. *Use these values in the Cartoon dialog*

8. Figure 10-9 shows the before and after comparison. When done,
    you can save as an .XCF file if you want to keep the file, or simply
    close it out.

Figure 10-9. *The before and after comparison*

Tutorial 29: Turn a Photo into a Warhol-Like Painting

In this lesson, we'll call on Posterize and the Cartoon filter once again, but we'll also use the Hue-Saturation dialog to vary the hues of the image to create a Warhol-like digital work of art.

1. Open the practice image *Ch_10_Tropical_Birds* in Glimpse.

2. Launch the Posterize dialog (Colors ➤ Posterize). This will reduce the number of colors in the image, making it look more like a drawing than a photograph.

3. Set the Posterize levels to 4, then click OK.

4. Launch the Cartoon filter (Filter ➤ Artistic ➤ Cartoon).

5. Use the settings as follows (shown in Figure 10-10):

    *   Mask radius—16.0

    *   Percent black—0.300

Figure 10-10. *Use these values in the Cartoon dialog*

6. Now we'll need to expand the canvas (Image ➤ Canvas)—once the dialog is open (see Figure 10-11), set the values as follows:

    • Width: 200%

    • Height: 200%

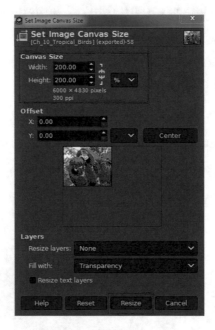

Figure 10-11. *Set the canvas size (width and height 200%)*

Click the Resize button after the size is set.

7. Create three duplicates of the background layer (Right-Click ➤ Duplicate Layer)—you'll need a total of four layers (Figure 10-12).

Figure 10-12. *Duplicate the background layer until there is a total of four*

8. Next, the layers will be put into place using the Alignment Tool; to
    do this, follow these steps (see Figure 10-13):

    -   Click the Alignment Tool icon.

    -   Click on top of the layer stack (indicated by a white node in each
        corner).

    -   Click the layer thumbnail of the layer you want to move, then use
        the appropriate distribute buttons to put each layer in place.

Figure 10-13. *Use the Alignment Tool to distribute each layer into place*

9. After the layers are in place, open the Hue-Saturation dialog
    (Colors ➤ Hue-Saturation). It will be used to change the hues in
    each layer.

10. Click the layer thumbnail of the bottom left layer to make it active,
    and set the Hue slider to −180, then click OK (Figure 10-14).

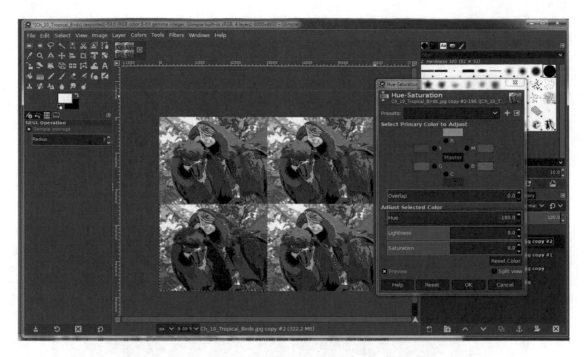

Figure 10-14. *Set the hue slider to −180 on the bottom left layer*

11. Repeat the steps on the top and bottom right side layers, using the values shown in Figure 10-15.

Figure 10-15. *The hue value slider settings for each layer*

12.   Figure 10-16 shows the final result. When done, you can save as an
.XCF file if you want to keep the file, or simply close it out.

Figure 10-16. *The final result*

Tutorial 30: Combine Two Images to Create a Digital Mural

In this final lesson, we'll combine two images in Glimpse to create a digital mural with a distressed look.

1. Open the practice image *Ch_10_Wooden_Fence* in Glimpse.

2. Open the practice image *Ch_10_Red_Flower* as a layer (File ➤ Open as Layers)—the image will open as a layer over the image of the wooden fence.

3. Open the Posterize dialog (Colors ➤ Posterize) and set the Posterize levels to 4 (Figure 10-17), then click OK.

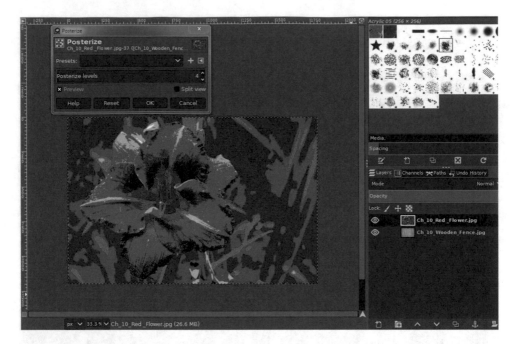

Figure 10-17. *The Posterize levels set to 4*

4. Change the layer blend mode to *Hard Light* (Figure 10-18).

Figure 10-18. *The layer blend mode changed to Hard Light*

5. Add a Layer Mask (Right-Click + Add Layer Mask)—when the dialog opens, initialize the Layer Mask to white (Figure 10-19).

Figure 10-19. *A Layer Mask initialized to white added to the layer*

6. Click the Paintbrush Tool (P) and select the Acrylic 01 brush tip.

7. Increase the brush size to about 850 pixels (between 800 and 900 is fine)—decrease the opacity to about 25% (Figure 10-20).

Figure 10-20. *The brush tip opacity set to almost 25% and the size changed to almost 870 pixels*

8. Click the layer mask thumbnail to make the layer mask active.

9. Place the brush tip in the area shown in Figure 10-21, and click once or twice—this will increase transparency where the brush is applied, and create a slight weatherworn look in that area of the image. You may want to experiment some by applying the effect in other areas or adjusting the brush opacity.

Figure 10-21. *Creating a slight "weatherworn" effect*

10. Now, we'll apply a slight blur to smooth the jagged edges caused by the Posterization effect. Click the layer thumbnail to make the layer active, then open the Gaussian Blur dialog (Filter ➤ Blur ➤ Gaussian Blur); set the X and Y blur values to 1.0, then click OK (Figure 10-22).

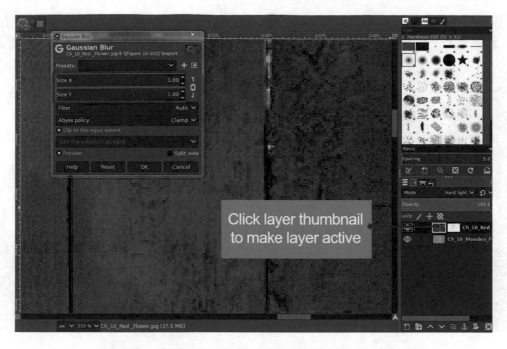

Figure 10-22. *Applying a slight blur to smooth out jagged edges*

11. Click the layer mask thumbnail to make the layer mask active.

12. Paint between the fence slats (with black) using a small, soft brush (4–7 pixels in diameter) to remove excess color that appears between the slats (Figure 10-23).

Figure 10-23. *With the layer mask active, paint between the slats to remove excess color*

13.   Figure 10-24 shows the final result. When done, you can save as an
      .XCF file if you want to keep the file, or simply close it out.

Figure 10-24. *The final result*

Chapter Conclusion

This chapter provided several lessons in which artistic filters (and other functions) were used to turn digital photos into works of art.

Here are the main topics that were covered:

- Turning a photo into a digital oil painting

- Turning a photo into a digital watercolor painting

- Turning a photo into a digital pen and ink drawing

- Turning a photo into a "Warhol-like" creation

- Combining two photos to create a digital mural

Congratulations! We covered a lot of ground in this book, and I hope you learned a lot. Glimpse is a powerful editing tool, and I encourage you to continue learning and growing using this program.

Index

A

Artistic filters
    digital mural, 237–242
    digital oil painting, 224, 225
    digital pen and ink drawing, 228–230
    digital watercolor painting, 226–228
    oil painting, 224
    Warhol-like painting, 231–234, 236
Auto White Balance, 103, 115–117

B

Brightening Teeth, 141–144
Brightness-Contrast dialog, 87–89

C

Clone Tool, 134, 150, 154
Color Balance dialog, 103–107
Color Temperature dialog, 107–110
Compositing images
    Clone Tool, 166
    Color Temperature dialog, 165, 166
    draw background option, 160, 161
    Foreground Select Tool, 158–160
    Move Tool, 164
    Quick Mask, 162, 163
    replacing backgrounds, 167, 168, 170–173
    scale tool, 163, 164
    stray pixels, 161, 162
    thumbnail preview, 158
    .XCF file, 167
Correcting exposure and contrast
    Brightness-Contrast dialog, 87–89
    correcting exposure and contrast, Exposure dialog, 80–82
    curves dialog, 94–97
    histogram, 91–94
    improving local tonality, 98–100
    levels dialog, 90, 91
    shadows-Highlights dialog, 83–86
Curves dialog, 94–97

D

Desaturate, 118–120, 123
Digital artwork
    raster vs. vector drawing, 195–198
    Retro TV Set, 212–215, 217–220, 222
    scenic Sunset, 207–211
    sunny Sky
        background color, 198, 199
        circular selection, 202
        dimensions and x/y resolutions, 200
        foreground color, 200, 201
        Gaussian Blur, 203, 204
        Lens Flare dialog, 206
        place guides, 200
        Smoke brush, 206
        white circle, 205
Digital mural, 237–242

Printed in the United States
By Bookmasters